P R E F A C E

Welcome to a no-nonsense guide that will tak
cityscapes. This book is your practical compani........ ...., ...
clear, concise instructions to elevate your urban explorations. It's designed for those
who value clear direction and efficient planning, ensuring you get the most out of
every city visit.

These pages contain a collection of cities, each with its own distinct personality and
charm. This guide has been meticulously designed to provide you with an
easy-to-follow itinerary that focuses on maximizing your experience in a limited time
frame. We cut through the noise to present the most important sights, sounds, and
tastes that define each destination.

Our approach is straightforward: we get right to the point. We recommend the
must-see attractions, the best restaurants, and the best routes to take in each city.
This book is about practicality and ease, saving you the trouble of sorting through
endless options and instead providing you with a clear path to a rewarding journey.

This guide is designed to help you dive straight into the heart of each city, whether
you are a seasoned traveler looking for efficiency or a first-time visitor looking for
straightforward advice. It's about making every minute count and spending your
valuable time experiencing the best that each urban landscape has to offer.

So gather your necessities, grab this guide, and prepare for a series of unforgettable
long weekend getaways. Let us set out on this adventure together, one city at a time.

LONDON, UNITED KINGDOM	BRUGES, BELGIUM
PARIS, FRANCE	KRAKOW, POLAND
ROME, ITALY	HELSINKI, FINLAND
BARCELONA, SPAIN	ST. PETERSBURG, RUSSIA
PRAGUE, CZECH REPUBLIC	ZAGREB, CROATIA
AMSTERDAM, NETHERLANDS	PORTO, PORTUGAL
BERLIN, GERMANY	GRANADA, SPAIN
VIENNA, AUSTRIA	RIGA, LATVIA
BUDAPEST, HUNGARY	WARSAW, POLAND
DUBROVNIK, CROATIA	LUXEMBOURG CITY, LUXEMBOURG
ATHENS, GREECE	LJUBLJANA, SLOVENIA
ISTANBUL, TURKEY	BELGRADE, SERBIA
MADRID, SPAIN	SOFIA, BULGARIA
FLORENCE, ITALY	TALLINN, ESTONIA
LISBON, PORTUGAL	SEVILLE, SPAIN
EDINBURGH, UNITED KINGDOM	VALENCIA, SPAIN
COPENHAGEN, DENMARK	GENEVA, SWITZERLAND
STOCKHOLM, SWEDEN	MILAN, ITALY
OSLO, NORWAY	NAPLES, ITALY
BRUSSELS, BELGIUM	BORDEAUX, FRANCE
ZURICH, SWITZERLAND	LYON, FRANCE
REYKJAVIK, ICELAND	NICE, FRANCE
VENICE, ITALY	GLASGOW, UNITED KINGDOM
DUBLIN, IRELAND	BUCHAREST, ROMANIA
MUNICH, GERMANY	THESSALONIKI, GREECE

London's
LONG WEEKEND ESCAPADE
A Whistle-Stop Tour for the Time-Crunched Traveler

Day 1: Dive into the Deep End of History

MORNING: THE TOWER OF LONDON

Stories of queens who were killed, beautiful gems, and, dare we say it, royal crimes await outside its stiff walls. Go deep, but don't stay there for too long. Henry VIII didn't, especially with his women.

LUNCH: BOROUGH MARKET

Feast on pies, fish and chips, and global delights. Remember, calories consumed on vacation don't count.

AFTERNOON: WESTMINSTER TOUR

Swing by Big Ben (yes, it might be covered in scaffolding, consider it London's version of a facial). Snap a photo outside the Houses of Parliament and whisper sweet nothings in Westminster Abbey's Whispering Gallery.

> ### CHARACTER OF THE CITY:
> London, how I miss you! Where the weather is as unpredictable as an EastEnders episode's plot twists, and where history and modernity share a cup of tea. The city is an eclectic mix of yesterday's grandeur and today's buzz, with a dash of quirky British charm thrown in for good measure.

EVENING: RIVER THAMES CRUISE

Float under illuminated bridges, waving at Shakespeare's Globe and the London Eye. Might as well see if the Thames' murky waters have improved(spoiler: they haven't).

Day 2: Art, Shopping, and That Thing Called Theatre

MORNING: THE BRITISH MUSEUM

Mummies, marbles, and treasures galore.
Don't spend too long with the Rosetta Stone; it won't teach you British slang.

LUNCH: COVENT GARDEN

Magicians, singers, and living statues, oh my! Grab a quick bite amidst entertaining chaos.

AFTERNOON: SHOPPING AT OXFORD STREET

Pro tip:
Guard your wallet!

EVENING: WEST END SHOW

From Les Mis to Lion King, there's drama, tears, and sequins waiting. Remember to applaud; those jazz hands aren't easy!

Day 3: Modern London with a Side of Royalty

MORNING: Tate Modern

It's edgy, it's contemporary, and some pieces might leave you scratching your head. Art, darling!

LUNCH: Camden Market

A mishmash of cuisines, vintage stalls, and edgy vibes. Tattoos optional.

AFTERNOON: Buckingham Palace

Wave to the Queen, and if she waves back, do buy a lottery ticket.

EVENING: Soho's Carnaby Street

Neon lights, music history, and trendy bars.
End your trip with a pint, or two!

NIGHT: Sky Garden

Overlook the city that never sleeps (or at least, takes short naps).
Sip on a cocktail and reminisce.

London in a long weekend? Mad, they said. Impossible, they claimed. But with this guide, not only will you capture the city's spirit, you'll also have a rollicking good time! Cheers, mate!

Paris Unpacked

A Long Weekend in the City of (not just) **Love**

Day 1: Icons, Heights, and Delightful Lights

MORNING: THE LOUVRE

A labyrinth of art treasures; from the smile of Mona Lisa to the armless beauty of Venus de Milo. Remember, the pyramid outside isn't a relic from ancient Egypt, just a modern touch!

LUNCH: Le Marais

Quaint cafes, cobblestones, and a sandwich 'jambon-beurre'. Yes, that's just ham and butter, but oh, what butter!

AFTERNOON: Eiffel Tower

Scale or elevator, get to the top! Paris stretches below, and your bragging rights stretch infinitely. If feeling cheeky, drop a "I can see my hotel from here!"

CHARACTER OF THE CITY:

Paris, where romance wafts through the air as frequently as the scent of freshly baked croissants. The city is a delightful cocktail of haute couture, historic boulevards, bohemian alleys, and the ever-present knowledge that you're a better person with a beret on.

EVENING: Seine River Cruise

As the sun sets, Paris glows (and it's not just the wine).
Glide past Notre-Dame, wave to lovers on bridges, and contemplate a moonlit swim (not recommended).

Day 2: Artists, Love Locks, and Gothic Blocks

MORNING: **Montmartre**

Meander where Picasso and van Gogh once did. The views from Sacre-Coeur are free; the art in the square, negotiable.

LUNCH: **Latin Quarter**

Dive into a world of shawarma, crepes, and philosophical debates about whether croissants are better than baguettes.

AFTERNOON: **Notre-Dame Cathedral**

Admire the Gothic beauty, and if Quasimodo rings a bell, it's probably just the hourly chimes.

EVENING: **Champs-Elysees & Arc de Triomphe**

Stroll the avenue, window shop (or splurge), and then climb to the top of the arch. Another panorama, because, why not?

Paris Unpacked

A Long Weekend in the City of (NOT JUST) **Love**

Day 3: Palatial Dreams and Bohemian Themes

MORNING: Versailles

A short train ride away. Grand halls, mirrored galleries, and gardens that might just put your backyard to shame.

LUNCH: Return to Paris & Head to Sainte-Chapelle

Bask in the kaleidoscope of its stained glass. It's like Instagram's filter, but from the 13th century.

AFTERNOON: The Left Bank

Bookshops, bohemians, and a world of intellectual legacy. Channel your inner Hemingway.

EVENING: Moulin Rouge

End with cancan dancers, plumes, and a show that's as French as a snooty poodle.

Paris in 72 hours? A whirlwind of elegance, history, and the occasional mime. Here's to the memories and the extra kilos from all those pastries. À la vôtre!

Rome in a Rush

72 Hours in the Eternal (Yet, Surprisingly Compact) City

Day 1: Roaming with the Romans

MORNING: Colosseum

Enter the grand amphitheater. You can almost hear the chariots and... lions? Thankfully, today's biggest threat is dodging selfie sticks.

LUNCH: Trastevere

A maze of quaint alleyways brimming with trattorias. Order pasta, think about Julius Caesar, and ponder: Would he have liked carbonara?

> **Character of the City:**
>
> Rome: where ancient ruins meet Vespas, and where gelato is a legitimate food group. Dive into a city that's older than your grandma's recipes, but with flavors that remain ever youthful. Get ready to be seduced by la dolce vita, one cobblestone at a time.

AFTERNOON: Roman Forum & Palatine Hill

Walk among temples, arches, and basilicas. Try not to time travel; we still need you for Day 2.

EVENING: Piazza Navona

An evening stroll with fountains, street artists, and a delightful Roman buzz.

Day 2: Vatican Ventures & Shopping

MORNING: **Vatican Museums & Sistine Chapel**

Meet Michaelangelo's ceiling masterpiece.
Neck strain is a small price to pay for divine artistry.

LUNCH: **Near Castel Sant'Angelo**

Near Castel Sant'Angelo, where pizza
and panini vendors dot the streets.
Bless your taste buds!

AFTERNOON: **St. Peter's Basilica**

Climb the dome, absorb the view. Wonder if Romans felt the
same vertigo.

EVENING: **Via del Corso**

A shopping spree or window lust; either way, your bags or eyes will be full.

Day 3: Fountains, Steps, & Roman Whispers

MORNING: Trevi Fountain

Toss a coin, make a wish. Mostly wish for more time in Rome.

LUNCH: Campo de' Fiori

A market square turned food haven. The Romans did say,
"When in Rome, eat as the Romans do."

AFTERNOON: Pantheon

Step inside, look up. It's a concrete marvel even after
2,000 years. They sure don't make 'em like they used to.

EVENING: Spanish Steps

Sit, people-watch, and end your trip
with a gelato in hand. One scoop for
every day in Rome. Or maybe two.
Who's counting?

Rome wasn't built in a day, but with some swift sandals and this guide, you've conquered it in three! Arrivederci and buon viaggio! 🏛️🍷🇮🇹

Barcelona Blitz

Three Days in the City of Gaudí and Good Times

Day 1: Gothic Dreams and Sea Breezes

MORNING: Gothic Quarter

Wander the medieval maze. Stumble upon ancient Roman walls, hidden courtyards, and perhaps a tapas bar or three. Remember, it's never too early for patatas bravas in Barcelona.

LUNCH: La Boqueria Market

Dive into a sensory overload. Jamón, cheese, olives, and more - every bite is a fiesta for your taste buds.

AFTERNOON: Barceloneta Beach

Sun, sea, and sand right in the city. Don't forget to check out the funky sculptures and artistic sandcastles.

EVENING: El Raval

Tapas crawl! As they say, "Eat when you drink, drink when you eat." It's a cycle, embrace it.

CHARACTER OF THE CITY:

Paris, where romance wafts through the air as frequently as the scent of freshly baked croissants. The city is a delightful cocktail of haute couture, historic boulevards, bohemian alleys, and the ever-present knowledge that you're a better person with a beret on.

Day 2: Gaudí Galore

MORNING: SAGRADA FAMILIA

Marvel at Gaudí's unfinished symphony of architecture.
Mind-blowing from the outside, jaw-dropping from the inside.

LUNCH:

Grab a bite in the Eixample district. Modernist architecture pairs
well with Catalonian cuisine.

AFTERNOON: PARK GUELL

It's like stepping into a fairytale. Colorful, quirky, and
with views that scream, *"LOOK AT ME, I'M IN BARCELONA!"*

EVENING: PASSEIG DE GRACIA

Stroll, shop, and admire more of Gaudí's
masterpieces like Casa Batlló and Casa Milà.

Day 3: Mountains, Magic, and Montjuïc

MORNING: Montjuic

Start with a cable car ride. Once atop, explore the castle, gardens, and panoramic vistas of the city and sea.

LUNCH: El Poble-sec

A neighborhood bursting with charm and delicious eateries. Get ready to loosen that belt buckle.

AFTERNOON: Magic Fountain

Await the evening spectacle but in the meantime, appreciate the surrounding grandeur of Plaça d'Espanya and the National Palace.

Three days in Barcelona might feel like a flamenco dance – swift, colorful, and leaving you wanting more. Until next time, visca Barça! 🌍💭🇪🇸

EVENING: El Raval

Lights, music, water acrobatics. It's like Disneyland but with fewer mouse ears and more Cava.

Prague in a Pinch

A 72-hour Dance in the Fairytale City

Day 1: Medieval Meanders and Evening Amblers

MORNING: Prague Castle

An impressive complex with palaces, churches, and gardens. The changing of the guard is fun, but let's be real, it's no "Gangnam Style".

LUNCH: Near Mala Strana (Lesser Town)

Pop into a quaint café for some hearty goulash or svíčková.

AFTERNOON: Charles Bridge

With statues, artists, and perhaps a magician or two, this is more than just a way across the river. Watch out for selfie stick duels.

EVENING: Passeig de Gracia

Watch the Astronomical Clock's parade (every hour) and debate if it's worth the hype.

Spoiler: The surrounding architecture might just steal the show.

CHARACTER OF THE CITY:

Welcome to Prague, where the beer is cheaper than water, and every alley whispers tales from centuries past. With spires that reach for the skies and cobblestones that have seen the march of time, Prague offers charm that's straight out of a storybook (with a side of dumplings).

Day 2: Bohemian Rhapsodies and Artistic Flair

MORNING: VYSEHRAD

A historic fort with legends, lush greenery, and serene views of the Vltava River. Rumor has it, it's the birthplace of Prague.

LUNCH: NAPLAVKA

Riverside market vibes. Grab a Trdelník (spiral pastry) and pretend it's traditional. It's touristy, but oh so tasty!

AFTERNOON: JOSEFOV (JEWISH QUARTER)

Visit synagogues, the old Jewish cemetery, and absorb poignant tales of history.

EVENING: LETNA PARK

Grab a Pilsner and enjoy panoramic views of the city. Best paired with some contemplative sighs.

Day 3: Modern Marvels and Hidden Gems

MORNING: Dancing House

Nicknamed 'Fred and Ginger' because, well, it looks like it's dancing. Architecture gets funky in Prague too!

LUNCH: Wenceslas Square

Dive into Prague's contemporary heart. It's named after a duke, not a Christmas carol. Promise.

AFTERNOON: Park Guell

Discover quirky modern art installations, including the famous giant baby statues. Yes, you read that right.

EVENING: Petrin Hill

Conclude atop this serene spot. There's a mini Eiffel Tower here, because why should Paris have all the fun?

Three days, and you've waltzed through Prague's pages of history, culture, and yes, beer. Na zdraví and until the next fairy tale! 🏰🍺🇨🇿

Amsterdam Antics

Canals, Clogs, and Three Days of Charm

Day 1: Canal Chronicles and Golden Ages

MORNING: Anne Frank House

Step into the harrowing past. Pro tip: Book in advance to avoid the queues that can be longer than your aunt's storytelling sessions.

LUNCH: The Jordaan

Bohemian vibes meet hearty Dutch fare. Indulge in broodjes, haring, or if you dare, bitterballen.

AFTERNOON: Canal Cruise

See Amsterdam from its liquid roads. If you don't wave at least once to a random Dutch family having tea, you're doing it wrong.

EVENING: Dam Square

The pulsating heart of Amsterdam, flanked by the Royal Palace and buzzing street performers. Great place to practice your Dutch... by which we mean nodding and smiling.

CHARACTER OF THE CITY:

Enter Amsterdam, where bicycles rule the streets, canals mirror fairy-tale facades, and tulips aren't just for gardens but for hearts too. Here, the legacy of Van Gogh and Vermeer entwines with liberal modernity, creating an ambiance that's as rich as Dutch cheese and as lively as a night at the Red Light District (wink!)

Day 2: Art, Parks, and Culinary Sparks

MORNING: The British Museum

A feast for art lovers. Absorb post-impressionism, and then journey through Dutch history. Remember,

IT'S VAN GOGH, NOT VAN GO.

LUNCH: Foodhallen

An indoor food market with global delicacies. Perfect for those who can't decide if they're more in a sushi or taco mood.

AFTERNOON: Vondelpark

Amsterdam's green lung. Rent a bike, pedal like a local, and maybe—just maybe—don a floral crown.

DANCE BABY

EVENING:

Leidseplein

Cafes, bars, and the promise of Amsterdam nightlife. Dance, sip, repeat.

Day 3: Quirky Corners and Windowed Wonders

MORNING: Albert Cuyp Market

rom stroopwafels to vintage finds, this bustling market is a
treasure trove. Haggle politely, or just say "Dank je" a lot.

LUNCH: Rembrandtplein

Surrounded by statues and cafes, it's the perfect place to reflect on
Rembrandt's genius... or just how many cheeses you can fit in your
suitcase.

AFTERNOON: Red Light District

An iconic area that needs little introduction. Explore with an open mind and
a ready camera (but respect the no-photo zones).

EVENING: Brouwerij 't IJ

Wind down near a windmill at this local brewery. Toast to Amsterdam with
craft beers that give new meaning to the term "high spirits."

Three whirlwind days in Amsterdam, and you've sailed its canals, tasted
its treats, and maybe even befriended a few ducks. Tot ziens and keep
those bicycle dreams alive! 🚲💚🇳🇱

Berlin Blitz

Wall Murals, Currywurst, and *72 HOURS* **of Pure Buzz**

Day 1: Landmarks, Legends, and Late-Night Lures

MORNING: **BRANDENBURG GATE**

Start with Berlin's iconic symbol of unity. Rumor has it that if you don't take a selfie here, you've never really been to Berlin.

LUNCH: **MITTE DISTRICT**

Dive into a café culture that's as hip as your uncle's vinyl collection. Don't forget to try the ubiquitous currywurst!

AFTERNOON: **REICHSTAG BUILDING**

Absorb history and city views from its glass dome. Remember, reservations are a must—just like those for that trendy pop-up vegan bratwurst stand.

EVENING: **HACKESCHER MARKT**

Boutiques, bistros, and Berliner Weisse (a local beer). If it sounds too sophisticated, wait till you see the street art!

CHARACTER OF THE CITY:

Berlin: where history is inked on every corner, where techno beats pulse through the night, and where "quirky" is the standard dress code. It's a city of contrasts—once divided, now united, and always evolving. Prepare to be wooed by a mix of gritty street art, grandiose landmarks, and the spirit of reinvention.

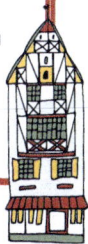

Day 2: War Stories, Wall Murals, and World-class Museums

MORNING: Berlin Wall Memorial

Walk the remnants of the Cold War, reading tales of escape and division. Don't worry, today's only wall-related challenge might be choosing a filter for your photos.

LUNCH: Prenzlauer Berg

Bohemian vibes with a side of falafel. Or Schnitzel. Or both. 😋

BERLIN DOESN'T JUDGE.

AFTERNOON: Museum Island

Five museums, one island. From the Pergamon Altar to Nefertiti's bust, it's a buffet of world history. Buffets are cool, right?

EVENING: Friedrichshain

Explore Berlin's edgy nightlife. Clubs in power plants, bars in basements—just an average Berliner evening.

Day 3: Modern Hubs, Historic Grubs, and Hipster Subs

MORNING: **Potsdamer Platz**

A hub of contemporary Berlin. Glass towers, shopping, and echoes of a once-divided city.

LUNCH: **Kreuzberg**

Dive into this melting pot neighborhood. Kebabs, burgers, vegan delights—it's the United Nations of food here.

AFTERNOON: **Checkpoint Charlie**

The famous crossing point between East and West Berlin. And yes, there's a museum too. Because, history.

Three days in Berlin feels like a thrilling sprint through epochs, ideologies, and a dash of döner kebab grease. Tschüss and keep those techno beats in your heart! 🎧🇩🇪

EVENING: **Holzmarkt**

Conclude your trip at this eclectic, riverside cultural space. Food, art, music—it's Berlin in a microcosm.

A Taste of Vienna

Imperial Palaces, DELIGHTFUL PASTRIES, **and a Fragrant Waltz**

Day 1: Imperial Indulgences and Melodic Muses

MORNING: Schonbrunn Palace

Start with a dose of imperial splendor. Explore its vast gardens, but maybe skip the maze unless you fancy playing hide and seek with history.

LUNCH: Naschmarkt

An iconic Viennese market. From falafels to Apfelstrudel, it's a culinary symphony. Just avoid humming while chewing!

AFTERNOON: State Opera House

Take a guided tour or, if you're feeling fancy, attend a matinée. Warning: Spontaneous waltzing might occur.

EVENING: Graben & Kohlmarkt

Elegant shopping streets begging for an evening stroll. Pick up some Mozartkugeln—chocolates, not mini composers.

CHARACTER OF THE CITY:

Vienna—where coffee is an art, music lingers in the air, and elegance is the everyday dress code. A city draped in Habsburg grandeur, enriched with artistic legacy, and sprinkled with Sachertorte sweetness. Time to twirl through Vienna's opulent corridors and contemporary coolness.

Day 2: Artsy Avenues and Coffeehouse Chronicles

MORNING: BELVEDERE PALACE

Immerse in baroque beauty and get up close with Gustav
Klimt's "The Kiss". But remember, no smooching the artwork!

LUNCH: CAFE CENTRAL

A historic coffeehouse. Indulge in a Melange
(Viennese coffee) and feel smarter just by
sitting where intellectuals once congregated.

AFTERNOON:
MUSEUMSQUARTIER

Dive into contemporary
art, culture, and some
funky lounging spots.
Perfect for those who
think outside the frame.

EVENING:
INNERE STADT (INNER CITY)

Explore narrow alleys, hidden
courtyards, and stumble upon
history at every turn. End with
a glass of Gemischter Satz,
because wine not?

Day 3: Gothic Grace, River Pace, and Prater Space

MORNING: St. Stephen's Cathedral

Gothic grandeur that'll have you craning your neck in wonder.
Climbing its tower might just burn off one of those pastries!

LUNCH: Spittelberg

A charming area with cobbled streets and cozy bistros. Perfect for
Schnitzel enthusiasts, and aren't we all?

AFTERNOON: Danube Island

A serene escape. Rent a paddleboat or simply enjoy riverside vibes.

EVENING: Prater

Vienna's amusement park. End your trip atop the Giant Ferris Wheel, and
wave at the entire city. They'll totally see you.

Three days in Vienna feels like a waltz through time—graceful,
romantic, and occasionally filled with cake. Auf Wiedersehen and let
the music play on! 🎻🎂🇦🇹

Budapest Binge

Thermal Baths, Tasty Tarts, and Danube Dreams

Day 1: Buda Bliss and Castle Kicks

MORNING: Buda Castle & Castle Hill

Rise and shine to panoramic city views and cobbled streets. You'll feel like royalty, minus the heavy crown.

LUNCH: Tabani Terasz

Hungarian cuisine with a view.
If you don't try goulash, did you even Budapest?

AFTERNOON: Fisherman's Bastion

An architectural wonder offering splendid Danube vistas. Watch out for photo-bombing pigeons They rule the roost

Character of the City:

Welcome to Budapest, where East meets West on the banks of the majestic Danube. Gothic spires rise alongside modern marvels, and history melds with hedonism. This is a place where you can sip coffee in a ruin bar by night and plunge into thermal waters by day. The city's dual nature, Buda and Pest, ensures twice the adventure!

EVENING: Gellert Hill

Catch a sunset like no other. Budapest bathed in golden hues? Check.

Day 2: Pest's Pleasures and Nibble Nights

MORNING: **PARLIAMENT BUILDING**

Iconic neo-Gothic elegance by the Danube. No politics, just pure aesthetics.

LUNCH: **CENTRAL MARKET HALL**

A gastronomic hub. Grab lángos and munch as you marvel at the market's buzz.

AFTERNOON: **ANDRASSY AVENUE & HEROES' SQUARE**

Stroll Budapest's Champs-Élysées. End at the square and give a nod to Hungarian legends.

EVENING: **JEWISH QUARTER & RUIN BARS**

Dive into the heart of Pest's nightlife. Szimpla Kert is legendary, but feel free to bar-hop because decisions are hard!

Day 3: Soaks, Sweets, and Sights on Streets

MORNING: Szechenyi Thermal Bath

Luxuriate in Europe's largest medicinal bath. Ducks get in free, so you might just make a feathery friend!

LUNCH: New York Cafe

Dubbed the "most beautiful café in the world". Consume pastries and opulence in equal measure.

AFTERNOON: Dohany Street Synagogue & Holocaust Memorial

Reflect and respect at Europe's largest synagogue.

EVENING: Danube River Cruise

Sail under twinkling bridges, cocktail in hand. If the river could applaud your Budapest binge, it would.

Three dazzling days in Budapest, and you've soaked, sighted, and savored. Viszlát and keep those thermal memories warm!

Dubrovnik Dash

Red Roofs, Ramparts, and Adriatic Allure

Day 1: Old Town Tales and Sunset Sails

MORNING: CITY WALLS

Start STop these iconic ramparts. The views? Think Lego sets come to life, only with fewer rogue pieces underfoot.

LUNCH: TAVERNA NOSTROMO

Nestled by the harbor, feast on seafood as fresh as the morning's gossip.

AFTERNOON: RECTOR'S PALACE & CULTURAL HISTORICAL MUSEUM

Dive into Renaissance grandeur and tales of the Dubrovnik Republic.

EVENING: BUZA BAR

A cliffside bar with views that'll knock your flip-flops off. Sip on Croatian wine as the sun dips into the Adriatic.

> **CHARACTER OF THE CITY:**
>
> Dubrovnik, or the "Pearl of the Adriatic", is a symphony of ancient stone, azure seas, and sun-dappled streets. A city that's as much a fortress as it is a fantasy realm (thanks, Game of Thrones), it promises tales of maritime might, medieval merriments, and more photo ops than you can shake a selfie stick at.

Day 2: Island Idylls and Medieval Modes

MORNING: Lokrum Island

A short ferry ride away. Wander botanical gardens, ruins, and make friends with peacocks and bunnies.

no, it's not a fairy tale

LUNCH: Prijeko Palace

Dine amidst history in the Old Town. The octopus salad is a revelation, much like realizing dragons aren't (sorry!).

AFTERNOON: Franciscan Monastery & Pharmacy

Meditate on monastic life, and maybe grab an ancient remedy from Europe's oldest still-operating pharmacy.

EVENING:

STRADUN

The city's main thoroughfare. Revel in its nocturnal charm, gelato in hand. Because gelato is always a good idea.

Day 3: Beach Bums, Cable Runs, and Culinary Fun

MORNING: BANJE BEACH

Dip your toes, or take the full plunge. Remember, tan lines may fade, but memories stay (so does sand in odd places!).

LUNCH: PANTARUL

Modern Dalmatian cuisine. Here, the truffle pasta has been known to elicit happy sighs.

AFTERNOON: DUBROVNIK CABLE CAR

Whisk up to Mt. Srđ for panoramic vistas. Peer over the edge and ponder if King's Landing could've handled a cable car.

EVENING: D'VINO WINE BAR

Conclude with Croatian vino and cheese. Because ending a trip without cheese is simply unheard of in storybooks.

Three days in Dubrovnik and you've sailed, strolled, and (possibly) sunburned. Dovidenja and may your next quest be equally enchanting!

Athenian Adventure

Ancient Acropolis, Alleys, and Hellenic Hype

Day 1: Temples, Tzatziki, and Time-traveling

MORNING: The Louvre

Begin on this iconic hill. Marvel at the Parthenon, try not to photobomb Athena's selfies.

LUNCH: Taverna Kaiti

Dive into Greek classics. Tip: The moussaka here might just make you break into spontaneous Zorba dancing.

AFTERNOON: Ancient Agora

Stroll where Socrates did. Muse over ancient markets and maybe grab a souvenir or two. (Alas, togas not included.)

EVENING: Plaka & Anafiotika

Wander these historic neighborhoods. Their narrow alleys and steps might just lead you to a minotaur. Or, more likely, a delightful café.

Character of the City:

Athens—where myths mingle with the modern, olive trees stand as sentinels of history, and every stone whispers tales of gods and heroes. Embrace a city that's as vibrant as its bougainvillea, and where philosophy isn't just studied—it's lived.

Day 2: Museums, Meanders, and Mediterranean Moods

MORNING: National Archaeological Museum

Dive into Greece's golden past. Just don't try to high-five the statues.

LUNCH: Avocado Cafe

A modern twist in the heart of history. For when you want a quinoa salad with your souvlaki.

AFTERNOON: Syntagma Square & Changing of the Guard

Watch evzones strut their stuff in traditional pleated skirts.
No giggling allowed!

EVENING: Monastiraki Square & Flea Market

Hunt for treasures, from antiques to unique trinkets. Haggling is an Olympic sport here!

Athenian Adventure

Ancient Acropolis, Alleys, and HELLENIC HYPE

DAY 3: BEACH BREEZES, BYZANTINE, AND BAKLAVA BLISS

MORNING: ATHENS RIVIERA & GLYFADA

Sun, sea, and sand. Poseidon might just give you a nod of approval.

LUNCH: BALUX CAFE

Seaside dining, Greek style. Try not to drop your feta in the sand.

AFTERNOON: BYZANTINE AND CHRISTIAN MUSEUM

A journey through Byzantine brilliance. It's like flipping through a very old, very ornate photo album.

EVENING: PSIRRI NEIGHBORHOOD

Dive into Athens' nightlife. End with baklava because sweet endings are always mythically good.

Three days in Athens and you've danced with history, dined like Dionysus, and probably debated democracy. Avrio and keep those heroic tales alive! 🏛️🇬🇷🍴

Istanbul Insights

Minarets, Markets, and BOSPHORUS BLISS

Day 1: Palaces, Prayers , Pide Perfection

MORNING: Hagia Sophia

Start with this architectural wonder, a basilica-turned-mosque-turned-museum. If walls could gossip, oh the tales they'd tell!

LUNCH: Karaköy Lokantasi

A taste of the contemporary in the historic Karaköy. Their mezze platter is more colorful than a sultan's tapestry.

AFTERNOON: Blue Mosque

Marvel at its cascading domes and 20,000 blue tiles. Tip: It's free, much like the goosebumps you'll get inside.

EVENING: Gulhane Park

A peaceful stroll amidst greenery and fountains. You might stumble upon Rumi writing verses (in spirit, of course).

> ### CHARACTER OF THE CITY:
>
> Istanbul: where East romances West, continents cozy up, and history is as layered as baklava. Sail between two worlds in a city where bazaars bustle, minarets pierce the skyline, and the aroma of Turkish tea beckons from every cor

Day 2: Bazaars, Bosphorus, and Baklava Bites

MORNING: GRAND BAZAAR

Over 500 years old and bursting with treasures. Got lost? That's part of the charm!

LUNCH: PANDELI

Located in the Spice Bazaar, it's an institution. Try the lamb shank; it's been praised since the Ottoman era.

AFTERNOON: BOSPHORUS CRUISE

Glide between Europe and Asia. Two continents in one afternoon? Check!

EVENING: BEYOGLU & ISTIKLAL STREET

The heart of modern Istanbul. Conclude with dessert at Hafız Mustafa—because when in Turkey, always end with sweets.

Day 3: Islands, Art, and Aromatic Ahhs

MORNING: Princes' Islands

No cars, just horse-drawn carriages and bicycles. It's like time traveling, with a sea breeze.

LUNCH: Heyamola Ada Lokantasi on Buyukada

Relish sea views and seafood. The calamari here could make Poseidon jealous.

AFTERNOON: Istanbul Modern

Gawk at Turkey's premier collection of contemporary art. A dash of culture with your kebab, perhaps?

EVENING: Ortakoy

Iconic views of the Bosphorus Bridge and the Ortaköy Mosque. Round off with a stuffed baked potato from a street vendor—because carbs amidst culture is just how Istanbul rolls.

Three days in Istanbul, and you've journeyed through empires, cruised continents, and indulged in treats that might just make you sing like a muezzin. Hoşça kal and cherish those Bosphorus breezes! 🚢🏛️🌀

Madrid
puerta de Europa
edificio telefonico
Royal Palace
PLAZA DE ISABEL II
Plaza de Cibeles
Alcala Gate
Plaza Mayor
hola
COFFEE
puerta de toledo
N
W
E
S

Captivating Madrid

Artistic Treasures, Bustling Mercados, MIDNIGHT FESTIVITIES Unveiled

DAY 1: PALACES, PLAZAS, AND PINCHOS

MORNING: PALACIO REAL

Roam the opulent rooms of Spain's Royal Palace. Question
your life choices for not being born into royalty.

LUNCH: MERCADO DE SAN MIGUEL

A market bursting with Spanish flavors.
From olives to oysters, it's a tapas
treasure trove.

AFTERNOON: PLAZA MAYOR

Marvel at Madrid's grandest square. Beware
of matadors. Just kidding. Maybe.

EVENING: LA LATINA

Explore this old district. Tapas bar hopping
is mandatory. If your stomach doesn't
leave expanded, you're doing it wrong.

CHARACTER OF THE CITY:

Madrid is a sophisticated seductress.
She entices with art, lures with
gastronomy, and captivates with endless
energy. At its core, Madrid is pure
passion — for life, for love, for siestas,
and most certainly for fiestas.

Day 2: Artful Adventures and Avenues

MORNING: Museo del Prado

Dive into one of the world's greatest
art collections. From Goya to
Velázquez, it's a visual fiesta.

LUNCH: Casa Mono

Relish Madrid's modern culinary twists in this chic bistro.

AFTERNOON: Retiro Park

Row a boat, admire peacocks, or simply
lounge by the Crystal Palace in Madrid's

EVENING: Gran Via

Madrid's bustling avenue, perfect
for shopping and people-watching.
Also, contemplating why there
aren't more hours in a day.

Day 3: Malasaña Moseying and Midnight Munchies

MORNING: TEMPLO DE DEBOD

An Egyptian temple in Madrid? Believe it. It's also one of the best sunrise spots.

LUNCH: LA BICICLETA CAFE

A trendy spot in Malasaña. Ideal for hipster-watching and savoring artisanal (read: fancy) sandwiches.

AFTERNOON: MALASANA DISTRICT

Vintage shops, street art, and bohemian vibes. It's Madrid's Brooklyn, with more sangria.

EVENING: CHOCOLATERIA SAN GINES

No Madrid visit is complete without churros y chocolate, especially at midnight. Night owls, this is your edible dream.

Three days in Madrid and you've waltzed with masterpieces, feasted like a king (or queen), and perhaps even taken a siesta or two. ¡Hasta la vista! And remember, Madrid might be in the heart of Spain, but it's also likely to find a special place in yours. 🐾🇪🇸

Exploring Florence

Tuscan Art, Culinary Treasures, and Three Days in the Renaissance Heart

Day 1: Statues, Squares, and Sangiovese Sips

MORNING: Piazza della Signoria & Palazzo Vecchio

Begin in Florence's historic heart. Say "Buongiorno!" to the statues, especially Michelangelo's David (the replica) standing tall and proud.

LUNCH: Trattoria da Mario

Tucked away, it's a Florentine classic. The ribollita soup is as hearty as Tuscan tales.

AFTERNOON: Uffizi Gallery

Art lover or not, this place enchants. Room after room of Renaissance glory. Beware: Stendhal Syndrome (being overwhelmed by art) is a real thing here!

> **Character of the City:**
>
> Florence, or Firenze as the locals fondly call it, is where art isn't just in museums—it's in the very air. Imagine a city painted with Medici gold, brushed with Botticelli's strokes, and echoed with Dante's verses. Florence is that grand canvas of history, culture, and gastronomy.

EVENING: Ponte Vecchio

This iconic bridge sparkles at dusk. Jewelers here might convince you that Renaissance bling is very much in vogue.

Day 2: Domes, Doors, and Decadent Delights

MORNING: Florence Cathedral & Brunelleschi's Dome

Conquer the 463 steps. Your reward? Panoramic views and bragging rights.

LUNCH: Mercato Centrale

A culinary carnival. Perhaps some pecorino cheese, or how about a lampredotto sandwich? (Don't ask, just try!)

AFTERNOON: Bargello Museum & Palazzo Medici Riccardi

Marvel at sculptures and frescoes. The Medici family probably walks these halls at night... in spirit.

EVENING:

La Giostra

Dine like Florentine royalty. Their fiorentina steak? A carnivore's dream, and probably a cow's worst nightmare.

Day 3: Gardens, Galleries, and Gelato Galore

MORNING: Boboli Gardens

Lose yourself in manicured mazes. If you find an apple tree with a
talking serpent, maybe stick to the main paths.

LUNCH: All'Antico Vinaio

A sandwich institution. Their focaccia might just make you pen sonnets.

AFTERNOON: Pitti Palace

Dive deeper into the Medici dynasty. Each room oozes opulence
and "Oh my!" moments.

EVENING: Gelateria La Carraia

Because no day in Italy should end without gelato. Triple scoops are totally
justifiable; after all, you've been walking all day!

Three days in Florence and you've waltzed with artists, dined like dukes, and
probably tried speaking Italian with your hands. Arrivederci and remember,
every cobbled corner here has a story to whisper! 🎨🍷🇮🇹

Discover Lisbon

A Tapestry of Fado Melodies, Funicular Journeys, and Gastronomic Wonders

Day 1: Trams, Towers, and Tantalizing Tarts

MORNING: BELEM TOWER & JERONIMOS MONASTERY

Start with the icons. Hint: They're older than your grandma's favorite chair and twice as ornate.

LUNCH: TIME OUT MARKET

A foodie's dream. From traditional bacalhau to modern vegan delights, it's Lisbon on a plate.

AFTERNOON: TRAM 28 RIDE

Hop on this historic tram that squeaks through Lisbon's most scenic spots. Hold on to your hats (and pastries)!

CHARACTER OF THE CITY:

Lisbon, perched on seven hills and gazing over the Tagus River, is a city of discoveries. It's where old trams trundle past grand plazas, and sorrowful fado music mingles with the salty sea breeze. There's an unpretentious charm here, a vibe that hums to the tune of soulful serenades and sardine-scented alleyways.

EVENING: ALFAMA DISTRICT

Wander the oldest part of the city, then settle in a local tasca for fado. It's soulful, melancholic, and may induce goosebumps.

Day 2: Castles, Commerce, and Codfish Croquettes

MORNING: Castelo de Sao Jorge

A hilltop fortress with sprawling city views.
Your camera will beg for mercy.

LUNCH: Cervejaria Ramiro

Seafood galore. The garlic prawns? They're the stuff of legends.

AFTERNOON: Baixa & Chiado

Dive into the heart of Lisbon's shopping
and cultural districts. Window shop or
wallet shop—your choice!

EVENING: Bairro Alto

A maze of bars and nightlife. Lisbon's pulse
quickens here, and so will yours.

Day 3: Parque Perusing, Panoramas, and Portuguese Pour-overs

MORNING: Parque das Nacoes

A modern side of Lisbon with futuristic architecture and a serene riverside setting.

LUNCH: Ponto Final

Across the river in Almada, dine with a view of the entire Lisbon skyline.

ORDER THE FISH.
TRUST US.

AFTERNOON: LX Factory

An industrial complex turned creative hub. Art, boutiques, and hipster vibes. Yes, you can get a pour-over coffee here.

EVENING: Park Bar

End on a rooftop with a cocktail in hand and the city at your feet. As the sun sets, toast to Lisbon's age-old allure.

Three days in Lisbon, and you've journeyed through history, tapped your feet to fado, and considered opening a pastel de nata bakery back home. Até logo! And remember, Lisbon lingers- in your memories, and quite possibly, on your taste buds. ✨🐟

Enchanting Edinburgh

Castles, Closes, and 72 HOURS **of Ceilidh-ing**

Day 1: St. Royal Mile, Ramparts, and…Riddles?

MORNING: EDINBURGH CASTLE

Perched upon an extinct volcano, this fortress offers history with a side of panoramic views. Don't miss the Crown Jewels!

LUNCH: THE WITCHERY BY THE CASTLE

With a name like that, expect an atmospheric meal in a historic setting. The steak tartare is bewitchingly good.

AFTERNOON: ROYAL MILE

Walk this historic stretch from castle to palace. Peek into closes (alleys) and courtyards. Every stone has a story here.

EVENING: THE REAL MARY KING'S CLOSE

Delve beneath the city streets for tales of old Edinburgh. Spooky? Aye. Fascinating? Double aye.

CHARACTER OF THE CITY:

Edinburgh is a city draped in history and shrouded in myths. Gothic spires rise above cobbled streets, while tales of knights, poets, and the occasional ghost echo through its alleyways. One moment you're atop an ancient volcano in the heart of the city, the next, you're diving deep into underground vaults. It's part fairy tale, part history lesson, and wholly enchanting.

Day 2: Palaces, Peaks, and Pints o' Ale

MORNING: HOLYROOD PALACE

The Queen's official Scottish residence. Admire the grandeur and ponder on swapping your apartment for a palace.

LUNCH: CLARINDA'S TEAROOM

A cozy spot for traditional Scottish fare. Think scones, clotted cream, and tea. Pinkies up!

AFTERNOON: ARTHUR'S SEAT

Hike up this ancient volcano in the heart of the city. The view? Edinburgh in all its glory. The feeling? Triumphant.

EVENING: THE ROYAL OAK

A traditional pub where folk music reigns supreme. Order a pint, tap your foot, and let the fiddles carry you away.

Day 3: Gardens, Galleries, and Ghostly Ghouls

MORNING: **Princes Street Gardens**

Stroll these picturesque gardens. If you see a squirrel wearing a kilt, you've been in Scotland too long.

LUNCH: **Scran & Scallie**

Gourmet Scottish grub in a pub setting. The haggis? It's not scary; it's scrumptious.

AFTERNOON: **Scottish National Gallery**

Dive into Scotland's art treasures. From Renaissance to Impressionists, it's a visual feast.

EVENING: **Greyfriars Kirkyard**

End with a ghost tour in this historic graveyard. Why? Because Edinburgh's tales aren't just in the past; they're in the afterlife too.

Three days in Edinburgh and you've stormed castles, danced with phantoms, and perhaps picked up a Scottish lilt. Cheerio! And remember, Edinburgh isn't just a city; it's an experience best narrated with a brogue and a twinkle in the eye. 🏰👻

Copenhagen Charms
Waterways, Royal Wonders, and a Weekend of Danish Deligh

Day 1: Palaces, Pedals, and Pastries

MORNING: Rosenborg Castle

Dive straight into Danish royalty. Beware of the throne room—it might just inspire you to buy a crown.

LUNCH: Torvehallerne

A bustling market where flavors dance. A smørrebrød (open sandwich) is mandatory.

AFTERNOON: Nyhavn

Stroll along this iconic canal. Those colorful houses? Probably made of LEGO (well, not really, but one can dream).

CHARACTER OF THE CITY:
Copenhagen- where fairy tales flirt with futuristic design, bicycles rule the roads, and 'hygge' (coziness) isn't just a word, it's a way of life. This city is a blend of old-world charm and modern, sustainable living, all wrapped up in one delightful Danish package.

EVENING: Tivoli Gardens

The world's second-oldest amusement park. Walt Disney found inspiration here; you might just find your inner child.

Day 2: Modern Museums, Mermaids, and Moreish Meals

MORNING: National Museum of Denmark

A journey through Viking helmets to modern artworks. No, you can't try on the Viking attire.

LUNCH: Copenhagen Street Food on Paper Island

Food trucks and waterside views. Go global with the menu; stay local with the beer.

AFTERNOON: The Little Mermaid Statue

Say hello to Denmark's most famous lady. She's smaller than you'd expect but captures a big place in your heart.

EVENING: Freetown Christiania

This self-proclaimed autonomous neighborhood is eclectic and colorful. Remember, photos aren't always appreciated, so soak in the memories.

Day 3: Design, Districts, and Danish Desserts

MORNING: **Designmuseum Danmark**

Dive into Danish design. Those iconic chairs?
More comfortable than a Viking's bed.

LUNCH: **Aamanns1921**

Masterful modern Danish cuisine. Each plate is like a canvas; you're
allowed to play with this kind of art.

AFTERNOON: **Stroget Shopping District**

Shop or window shop in one of Europe's longest pedestrian streets.
Your wallet might feel lighter but your heart, much fuller.

EVENING: **La Glace**

End with Denmark's oldest confectionery. Their cakes? Hans
Christian Andersen probably wrote about them (or should have).

Three days in Copenhagen and you've cozied up with culture, dined like Danish royalty, and probably contemplated moving here permanently. Farvel and keep the 'hygge' alive wherever you go!

Stockholm Elegance

Archipelago Charms, Creative Vibes, and A Journey Through Design Excellence

Day 1: Royal Residences, Riveting Routes

MORNING: Gamla Stan

Delve deep into Stockholm's Old Town. Meander through medieval streets, and whisper hello to ghosts of Vikings past.

LUNCH: Chokladkoppen

Nestled in Gamla Stan's heart, indulge in Swedish treats, especially the cinnamon buns. Coffee's the sidekick here.

Character of the City:

Stockholm gracefully sprawls across 14 islands, knit together by bridges and ferries. It's a city where cutting-edge design dances with deep-rooted history, where regal palaces rub shoulders with innovative museums, and where sunlight (or moonlight) shimmers on tranquil waters. Welcome to the Venice of the North.

AFTERNOON: The Royal Palace

A royal bonanza of opulent chambers and regal guards. Witness the Changing of the Guard – it's pomp and pageantry, Stockholm style.

EVENING: Sodermalm

The city's bohemian hub. Think artists, hip bars, and panoramic city views. Stockholm's cooler than your average capital.

Day 2: Vasa Ventures, Viking Ventures

MORNING: PARLIAMENT BUILDING

Gawk at a fully intact 17th-century ship. It sank on its maiden voyage. Oops. It's history's most magnificent fail.

LUNCH: OAXEN SLIP

Nordic bistro on Djurgården island. Savour sustainable dishes amidst nautical charm.

AFTERNOON: ABBA THE MUSEUM

Embrace your dancing queen (or king) in this interactive tribute to Sweden's pop sensation.

EVENING: FOTOGRAFISKA

A contemporary photography museum that's as much about the art as it is about the views from the top-floor restaurant.

Day 3: Modern Museums, Midnight Sun Moments

MORNING: Moderna Museet

Plunge into a world of modern and contemporary art. Picasso? Check. Matisse? Double-check.

LUNCH: Rosendals Tradgard

A garden cafe on Djurgården. Greenhouses, fresh produce, and organic allure. Photosynthesize some happiness.

AFTERNOON: Skansen

The world's oldest open-air museum. From traditional crafts to Nordic animals, it's a Swedish smorgasbord.

EVENING: Nobel Prize Museum

Learn about laureates and their world-changing achievements. Then daydream about your own Nobel speech.

Three days in Stockholm and you've journeyed through history, danced with pop legends, and probably developed an obsession with Swedish design. Hej då! And remember, while the midnight sun might set on your Stockholm adventure, the memories will glow forever. 🍽️🎨➕

Oslo Odyssey

Majestic Fjords, Rich Folklore, and a Celebration of Fika and Culture

Day 1: Operatic Openings, Oceanic Outings

MORNING: Oslo Opera House

Begin with this architectural marvel that invites you to walk on its roof. No, really, it's encouraged!

LUNCH: Fiskeriet Youngstorget

Reel in the freshest seafood in this bustling market setting. The fish soup? A maritime hug in a bowl.

AFTERNOON: Akershus Fortress

Traverse this medieval castle and feel centuries of Norwegian history underfoot. Hope you're wearing your knight-approved sneakers.

> **CHARACTER OF THE CITY:**
>
> Oslo, the splendidly green capital of Norway, seamlessly weaves the natural with the urbane. From its iconic opera house resembling an iceberg to the dense forests encircling the city, Oslo is where eco-friendliness meets world-class culture. It's the epitome of Scandinavian sophistication, with a dash of Viking valor.

EVENING: Aker Brygge

A vibrant harbor promenade. Enjoy waterfront dining, shopping, and musing, "Should I buy that Viking helmet?"

Day 2: Munch Moments, Museum Meanders

MORNING: The Munch Museum

Immerse yourself in the world of Edvard Munch.
The Scream is just the beginning.

LUNCH: Ekebergrestauranten

Elevated dining (literally). Relish panoramic city views and dishes that are works of art themselves.

AFTERNOON: Viking Ship Museum

Unearth Norway's seafaring heritage.
Bonus: Feel like a Viking, minus the pillaging.

EVENING:

Mathallen Food Hall

A foodie paradise with a Norwegian twist. Sample local cheeses, cured meats, and yes, waffles. Because,

Day 3: Forested Forays, Fjord Frolics

MORNING: Frognerseteren

Dive into Nordmarka forest for hiking or skiing, depending on the season. Breathe. It's pure Norwegian air.

LUNCH: Lille Herbern

A hidden gem on a tiny island. Seafood by the fjord? Yes, please.

AFTERNOON: Vigeland Park

Admire over 200 sculptures by Gustav Vigeland. Humans in all their naked emotion. Literally.

EVENING: Ingens Gate

Dive into Oslo's hipster heartland. Craft beers, cool art, and chances to practice your "Skål!"

Three days in Oslo and you've harmonized with high culture, saluted to seafaring ancestors, and perhaps contemplated a new life as a fjord-side fisherman. Ha det! And remember, Oslo isn't just a city; it's a Norwegian narrative waiting to be lived. 🌲🎿✈️

Brussels Enchantment

Decadent Chocolates, City Charms, and a Whirlwind of ARTISTIC WONDERS

Day 1: Grandeur, Galleries, and Gastronomic Glee

MORNING: Grand-Place

Kickstart at Brussels' magnificent central square. Surround yourself with opulent guildhouses and a town hall that's basically architectural couture.

LUNCH: Chez Leon

Dive into mussels in Brussels. It's like Netflix and chill, but tastier.

AFTERNOON: Manneken Pis

Meet the tiny bronze boy taking a, well, pee. Why? It's Brussels, darling.

EVENING: Delirium Cafe

oasting over 2,000 beers, it's hop heaven. Remember: sip responsibly, giggle limitlessly.

CHARACTER OF THE CITY:

Brussels, Belgium's capital, is an eclectic fusion of old-world allure and modern-day governance. Known as the de facto capital of the European Union, Brussels has a cosmopolitan flair balanced with a rich historical fabric. Plus, let's face it: This is probably the only city where a cheeky peeing statue is a national treasure.

Day 2: Regal Residences, Riotous Reliefs

MORNING: **Atomium**

Marvel at this atomic-age structure. The views from the top are explosively good.

LUNCH: **Maison Antoine**

Fries before guys. Or gals. Or anything, really.
This joint's frites are legendary.

AFTERNOON: **Royal Palace of Brussels**

Indulge in some royal reconnaissance. If walls could talk, these would have a posh accent.

EVENING: **Comic Strip Route**

Wander the city discovering murals of iconic comic characters. Tintin, anyone?

Day 3: Chocolate Charms, Cherished Chapels

MORNING: MAGRITTE MUSEUM

Surrender to the surreal in this tribute to Rene Magritte, Belgium's iconic artist.

LUNCH: CHOCO-STORY BRUSSELS

A museum devoted to chocolate. Eat your way through history. Literally.

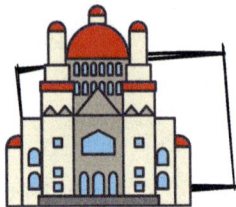

AFTERNOON: ST. MICHAEL AND ST. GUDULA CATHEDRAL

A Gothic masterpiece. Light a candle, or simply bask in its divine beauty.

EVENING: RUE DES BOUCHERS

A bustling lane of eateries. Dive into culinary Brussels, one bite at a time.

Three days in Brussels, and you've wined, dined, and perhaps even serenaded a bronze statue. Au revoir! And remember, in the world of chocolates and waffles, Brussels is the golden ticket. 🍫🧇🍟

ZURICH

Zippy Zurich

Lakes, Landmarks, and 72 Hours of LUSH LIVING

DAY 1: LIVELY LANES, LOVELY LAKES

MORNING: BAHNHOFSTRASSE

One of the world's ritziest streets. Shop, gawk, or simply strut. Feeling fancy yet?

LUNCH: ZEUGHAUSKELLER

Dine in a historic armory. Swiss cuisine served with a side of history. No swords at the table, please.

AFTERNOON: LAKE ZURICH

Stroll along the promenade or opt for a tranquil boat ride. The ducks are friendly, but they're watching your sandwich.

EVENING: ALTSTADT (OLD TOWN)

Dive into a labyrinth of historic alleyways. Cobblestones underfoot, stories in every nook.

CHARACTER OF THE CITY:

Zurich, the pulsating heart of Switzerland, effortlessly marries its roles as a global banking capital with its rich, historic charm. Nestled beside the glistening waters of Lake Zurich and framed by snow-capped mountains, this city serves both urban sophistication and scenic splendors. Oh, and did we mention chocolate?

Day 2: Artful Ambles, Alpine Admires

MORNING: Kunsthaus Zurich

Marvel at masterpieces ranging from medieval icons to modern artworks. Art snob hat optional.

LUNCH: Cafe Schober

Indulge in pastries in this baroque coffeehouse. Calories don't count in historic settings, right?

AFTERNOON: Uetliberg Mountain

A short train ride and hike rewards you with panoramic city views. Who needs a drone?

EVENING: Thermalbad & Spa Zurich

Bathe in thermal waters atop an old brewery. It's relaxation, Zurich style.

Day 3: Church Chimes, Chocolate Cheers

MORNING: GROSSMUNSTER

Climb the towers of this iconic double-spired church.
Burn calories, gain views.

LUNCH: SWISS CHUCHI

Raclette, fondue, and hearty Swiss delights. Did someone say
cheese avalanche?

AFTERNOON: LINDT HOME OF CHOCOLATE

The name says it all. Dive into cocoa-filled wonder.
Yes, there's a tasting room.

EVENING: ZURICH OPERA HOUSE

Conclude with an evening of
cultural opulence. Standing
ovations encouraged.

Three days in Zurich, and you've swayed with
symphonies, communed with chocolates, and
perhaps contemplated opening a Swiss bank account
for all the souvenirs. Auf Wiedersehen! And
remember, while the Swiss watch may tick forward,
Zurich memories are timeless. 🕐🍫✚

Reykjavik Wonders

Geothermal Marvels, Mythical Tales, and A Journey Through Iceland's **Natural Splendor**

Day 1: Cultural Chronicles, Culinary Conquests

MORNING: Hallgrimskirkja Conquests

Start at this iconic church. Its tower offers sweeping views of the city's rainbow-colored roofs.

LUNCH: Bæjarins Beztu Pylsur

Devour a famous Icelandic hot dog. The name translates to "the town's best hot dog," and they aren't kidding.

AFTERNOON: Harpa Concert Hall

Gawk at this architectural wonder. The geometric glass panels seem to dance in the sunlight.

EVENING: Laugavegur

Delve into Reykjavik's main shopping street. Endless boutiques, bars, and a chance to get your elf-spotting glasses.

Character of the City:

Reykjavik, though petite in size, is mammoth in spirit. This colorful city, dotted with quaint houses, is a hub of creativity, ancient sagas, and nature's marvels. Amidst biting cold and dancing Northern Lights, Reykjavik's warm-hearted locals welcome you to a saga you'll never forget.

Day 2: Natural Nooks, Nighttime Novelties

MORNING: GOLDEN CIRCLE TOUR

This isn't just a drive—it's an epic quest. Gushing
geysers, tumbling waterfalls, and more await.

LUNCH: FRIDHEIMAR

A tomato farm in the middle of nowhere. Fresh
tomato soup under a greenhouse roof? Heavenly.

AFTERNOON: THINGVELLIR NATIONAL PARK

A UNESCO site where tectonic
plates meet. Walk between

BECAUSE
WHY NOT?

EVENING:

NORTHERN LIGHTS

If visiting during the right season, catch this celestial ballet.
Nature's disco, no entry fee.

Day 3: Blue Bliss, Breezy Bylanes

MORNING: BLUE LAGOON

Bathe in milky blue geothermal waters. It's like a spa day, but on an otherworldly planet.

LUNCH: REYKJAVIK ROASTERS

Warm up with artisanal coffee and pastries. The cinnamon buns? An Icelandic hug on a plate.

AFTERNOON: SUN VOYAGER SCULPTURE

Ponder at this striking ode to the sun. Snap a pic, or ten.

EVENING: KOL RESTAURANT

Dive into contemporary Icelandic cuisine. Puffin, fermented shark, or just a classic fish dish? The icy culinary world is your oyster.

Three days in Reykjavik, and you've hobnobbed with elves (maybe), been kissed by geothermal mists, and perhaps even busted a move under the auroras. Bless í bili! And remember, while the geysers may erupt and recede, Reykjavik memories simmer forever.

Vivacious Venice

Gondolas, Grandeur, and 72 Hours of Gelato-Induced Grins

Day 1: St. Mark's, Serenades, and Seafood Surprises

MORNING: St. Mark's Square & Basilica

Begin in Venice's beating heart. Feed the pigeons; they're almost as historic as the square itself.

LUNCH: Osteria Al Portego

A local haunt. The cicchetti (small dishes) are bite-sized pieces of Venetian heaven.

AFTERNOON: Doge's Palace

Dive into Venetian grandeur. Those walls have seen more drama than a Shakespearean play.

EVENING: Gondola Ride

Glide through canals as gondoliers serenade. Cliché? Maybe. Magical? Absolutely.

CHARACTER OF THE CITY:

Venice – a dreamy maze where streets are canals, vehicles are boats, and every turn is a serenade. Floating atop the Adriatic's embrace, Venice is where time seems suspended, and every reflection holds a millennia-old tale.

Day 2: Islands, Art, and Aperitivo Hours

MORNING: Murano & Burano

Visit these islands for lace and glass wonders. Leave with a lighter wallet and heavier suitcase.

LUNCH: Trattoria al Gatto Nero on Burano

Relish the freshest seafood. The fish practically jumped onto your plate!

AFTERNOON: Peggy Guggenheim Collection

Contemporary art in a palazzo setting. Picasso in a palace? Only in Venice.

EVENING:

Campo Santa Margherita

A buzzing square. Enjoy an aperitivo, watch the world float by, and debate about learning Italian full-time.

Day 3: Bridges, Books, and Bacari Bars

MORNING: RIALTO BRIDGE & MARKET

Shop and snap photos atop Venice's most iconic
bridge. Barter like a Venetian of yore.

LUNCH: CANTINA DO SPADE

Near Rialto, this bacaro (wine bar) serves divine cicchetti. If Venice was
a flavor, this would be it.

AFTERNOON: LIBRERIA ACQUA ALTA

A bookstore where books float in gondolas. They take their water
theme seriously!

EVENING: BACARETO DA LELE

End with local wine and tapas-sized treats. Raise a toast to Venice, the city
that has your heart (and maybe a bit of your wallet).

Three days in Venice, and you've danced with dukes, feasted on lagoonal
delights, and probably contemplated buying a gondola. Arrivederci!
Remember, Venice is best described not in words, but in sighs. 🎨🏙️

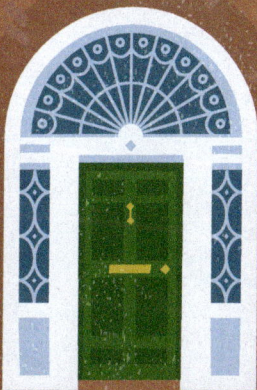

Dublin Delights

Mythical Charms, Literary Treasures, and a Taste of Irish Elixir

Ah, Dublin! Where tales flow as freely as the Guinness, where the streets hum with history, and where every pub corner seems to conceal a poet or a storyteller. Don your finest green attire and let's dive into this Gaelic gem with gusto. Sláinte!

Day 1: Histories, Hooves, and Hoppy Delights

MORNING: Trinity College & The Book of Kells

Begin with this iconic campus. Marvel at the Book of Kells, an illuminated manuscript that even predates your grandma's diary.

LUNCH: Queen of Tarts

Indulge in savory pies and dreamy desserts. It's so good, you might even write a ballad about it.

AFTERNOON: Dublin Castle

Dive deep into Dublin's history. The castle, part medieval, part Georgian, is 100% fascinating.

EVENIGHT: Temple Bar

Wander Dublin's cultural quarter. Pubs, music, and a chance to find your very own four-leaf clover.

CHARACTER OF THE CITY:

Dublin, the jovial Irish capital, is a seamless blend of profound history and infectious energy. From the rebellious tales of yore to the poetic fervor that infuses its streets, Dublin invites you with a wink, a smile, and a hearty toast.

Day 2: Gaols, Graftons, and Goblets of Gold

MORNING: Kilmainham Gaol

Visit this historic prison. Learn about rebellions, renaissances, and why it's a bad idea to misbehave in Dublin.

LUNCH: Gallagher's Boxty House

Taste Boxty, a traditional potato pancake. Potatoes in a pancake? Pure

AFTERNOON: Grafton Street

Shopping and street performers galore. Pick up a tin whistle and join the fray.

EVENING: Guinness Storehouse

Imbibe the story of Ireland's famous brew. And yes, there's a tasting session atop the Gravity Bar with panoramic city

Day 3: Bridges, Brogues, and Balladeer Evenings

MORNING: Dublin Zoo

Venture into one of the world's oldest zoos, nestled within the lush Phoenix Park.

WHO KNEW
DUBLIN HAD FLAMINGOS?

LUNCH: The Woollen Mills

Relish traditional fare with a modern twist. The pulled pork sandwich? A revelation.

AFTERNOON: Ha'penny Bridge & River Liffey Walk

Stroll along Dublin's iconic pedestrian bridge and the riverbanks of the Liffey. Poetic musings optional, but encouraged.

EVENING: Irish Whiskey Museum

Discover the golden history of Irish whiskey. Engage in spirited tales and tastings, and maybe, just maybe, decipher the age-old debate: whiskey or

NIGHT: O'Donoghue's

Round off with live traditional Irish music. It's the kind of place where a casual evening might morph into a legendary night of stories, songs, and serendipity.

With this spruced-up Day 3, you've truly embraced the Dublin spirit, wandering its streets, waterways, and warming your soul with its melodies. And as you depart, may your heart always have a touch of Irish rhythm and your step a Dubliner's sprightly spring! 🍀🇮🇪

Munich Magic

Royal Residences, Bavarian Treats, and a Whirlwind of Festive Spirit

Day 1: Royal Beginnings, Riveting Rhythms

MORNING: Nymphenburg Palace

Begin in the lap of Bavarian luxury. With its Baroque architecture and sprawling gardens, this palace might just give Versailles a run for its money.

LUNCH:
Viktualienmarkt

Munich's daily food market. Grab a weisswurst (white sausage), a pretzel, and embrace your inner Bavarian.

CHARACTER OF THE CITY:

Munich gracefully straddles the line between its rich history and a vibrant modern beat. Gothic spires rise alongside sleek skyscrapers, and beer gardens buzz beneath ancient trees. It's where tradition clinks mugs with innovation.

AFTERNOON: Marienplatz & Glockenspiel

The city's heart. Stick around for the Glockenspiel's delightful chime, where figures dance as if trying to impress the town's pigeons.

EVENING: Hofbrauhaus

An evening in Munich's most iconic beer hall.

⚠️ WARNING: SPONTANEOUS YODELING MIGHT OCCUR.

Day 2: Arts, Ales, and Alpine Stories

MORNING: **Alte Pinakothek**

Immerse in European art masterpieces. Think of it as Instagram, but from the Renaissance era.

LUNCH: **Augustiner Braustuben**

Local vibes, hearty meals, and beers that've been brewed since the 1300s. Ancient ale? Absolutely.

AFTERNOON: **Olympiapark**

Dive into the heart of Lisbon's shopping and cultural districts. Window shop or wallet shop—your choice!

EVENING: **Munchner Stadtmuseum**

Dive into Munich's story. And yes, there's an entire exhibit on beer. Priorities.

Day 3: Spiritual Spaces, Sparkling Sips

MORNING: FRAUENKIRCHE

Marvel at Munich's iconic twin-towered church. They say the devil once left a footprint here. Pop in and play

LUNCH: CAFE FRISCHHUT

Famous for its pastries and strudels. Pro tip: try the Schmalznudel, a sweet pastry that sounds like a magical spell.

AFTERNOON: ENGLISCHER GARTEN

One of the world's largest urban parks. Serene streams, traditional tea houses, and sometimes, surfers. Yes, surfers.

EVENING: GASTEIG CULTURAL CENTER

A buffet of culture – concerts, theater, and film. The perfect curtain call for our Munich merrymaking.

Three days in Munich, and you've tangoed with kings, sampled centennial brews, and perhaps learned a Bavarian jig or two. Auf Wiedersehen! And remember, while the beer might eventually leave your system, Munich memories linger indefinitely. 🍺🏰🇩🇪

Bewitching Bruges

Chocolates, Canals, and COBBLESTONE CHARMS

Day 1: MYSTIQUE, MARKETS, AND MEDIEVAL MARVELS

MORNING: THE MARKT

Begin your journey in Bruges' beating heart. Admire the colorful facades, but keep an eye out for the horse-drawn carriages. They don't have brakes... or maybe they just don't use them!

LUNCH: DE VLAAMSCHE POT

Dive into authentic Flemish cuisine. Their beef stew tastes like a medieval knight decided to become a chef.

AFTERNOON: BELFRY TOWER

366 steps to panoramic views. You'll huff, you'll puff, and you'll probably contemplate medieval fitness regimes.

CHARACTER OF THE CITY:

Bruges is like stepping into a medieval dreamscape—gingerbread-style houses, echoing footsteps on ancient cobblestones, and the soft murmur of canal waters. Here, every corner promises a story, every shadow might hide an elf, and every chocolate shop is... well, heaven.

EVENING: BOURGOGNE DES FLANDRES BREWERY

Because in Bruges, the answer to "Beer or IS ALWAYS "BEER, OF COURSE!"

Day 2: Chocolates, Chapels, and Charming Canals

MORNING: THE CHOCOLATE LINE

A Willy Wonka-esque wonderland by chocolatier Dominique Persoone. Expect flavors like cola, sake, and fried onions. Adventurous taste buds, activate!

LUNCH: 'T ZWART HUIS

Art Deco vibes and delectable dishes. Bonus: the jazz music might just transport you to the 1920s.

AFTERNOON: CANAL TOUR

Glide through Bruges' arteries, waving at envious ducks and possibly befriending a swan or two.

EVENING: BASILICA OF THE HOLY BLOOD

Admire the vial said to contain a drop of Christ's blood. No vampires allowed, though. We checked.

Day 3: Artistic Alleys, Ancient Abbeys

MORNING: GROENINGEMUSEUM

Renaissance masterpieces, a sprinkle of modern art, and maybe a paintbrush-wielding ghost. Not confirmed, but highly suspected.

LUNCH: LI O LAIT

A quirky café. Because amidst all the history, a touch of hipster never hurt anyone.

AFTERNOON: BEGUINAGE

A peaceful oasis once home to the beguines, pious women who were kind of like medieval nuns but with fewer rules.

EVENING: 2BE BEER WALL

End with a literal wall of beer options. It's like a library, but instead of "Shhh," the librarian says, "Cheers!"

Three days in Bruges feels like a dance with time—swaying between centuries, twirling amidst tales, and always, always ending on a sweet note (probably chocolate). As you bid adieu, remember: Bruges isn't just a city; it's a chocolate-coated, canal-crossed dream.

Kraków Kaleidoscope

Regal History, Chivalrous Tales, and a Cultural Mosaic Unveiled

Day 1: Spires, Squares, and Salt Mines

MORNING: WAWEL ROYAL CASTLE

Kick off with a royal start. A former residence of Polish monarchs, this castle has seen its share of coronations, feasts, and perhaps a dragon's fiery tantrum.

LUNCH: PIEROGI HEAVEN

Literally, that's the place's name. And yes, the dumplings are divinely delicious.

AFTERNOON: WIELICZKA SALT MINE

Venture into this underground marvel. Remember, if you lick the walls, you're just "tasting history." 😉

EVENING: KAZIMIERZ DISTRICT

Wander through the Jewish quarter, absorbing its rich heritage. Maybe whistle a tune from Fiddler on the Roof. It feels apt.

CHARACTER OF THE CITY:

Kraków is a canvas painted with strokes of history, folklore, and vibrant modern life. With its medieval squares and Gothic spires, it feels like a place where you might stumble upon a knight's duel or a wizards' convention.

Day 2: Tales, Taverns, and Timeless Traditions

MORNING: Main Market Square & St. Mary's Basilica

Marvel at Europe's largest medieval square and catch the hourly trumpet call from the church's tower. Legend has it the melody breaks abruptly to commemorate a trumpeter shot while warning of a Mongol invasion.

LUNCH: Morskie Oko

No, not the lake in the Tatra Mountains. It's a traditional Polish tavern in the city. Grab a bigos stew and revel in the rustic ambiance.

AFTERNOON: Oskar Schindler's Factory

A moving reminder of WWII's history and the heroics of an unlikely savior.

EVENING:

BARAWKA

Indulge in a modern twist on Polish cuisine. Warning: may cause spontaneous exclamations of "Smacznego!"

Day 3: Artistic Ambles, Aerial Views

MORNING: MOCAK MUSEUM OF CONTEMPORARY ART

See the modern side of Kraków. Ponder, appreciate,
and maybe tilt your head a bit for that artsy effect.

LUNCH: ALCHEMIA OD KUCHNI

A fusion of flavors in the heart of Kazimierz. Perfect for those
"I can't decide what I want" moments.

AFTERNOON: KOSCIUSZKO MOUND

Climb this man-made hill for panoramic views. Legend says it's made of soil
from various battlefields where national hero Tadeusz Kościuszko fought.

EVENING: PIWNICA POD BARANAMI

End your journey in a cellar cabaret that has played host to the city's
bohemian life for decades.

Three days in Kraków is like thumbing through a living history book,
with a touch of magic on every page. As you depart, remember:
Kraków isn't just a place; it's a tale waiting to be told. 🏰🗡🥐

Helsinki

Northern Lights & DESIGN DELIGHTS

Day 1: Sea Breezes & Modern Designs

MORNING: Suomenlinna Sea Fortress

Start your day with a ferry ride to this UNESCO World Heritage site. Built on six islands, this fortress offers a glimpse into Finland's maritime history.

LUNCH: Market Square

Dive into local flavors with fresh fish dishes or reindeer meatballs. Look out for seasonal berry treats!

AFTERNOON: Design District

Wander through boutiques and galleries showcasing Finland's renowned design heritage. From Marimekko fabrics to Iittala glassware, it's a designer's dreamland.

EVENING: Loyly Sauna

Embrace the Finnish tradition! This contemporary wooden sauna by the sea allows you to alternate between steamy interiors and brisk sea dips.

CHARACTER OF THE CITY:

Nestled by the Baltic Sea, Helsinki is the epitome of Nordic cool. A city where modernist architecture meets a rich maritime history, and where every street whispers tales of the sea, saunas, and Sibelius.

Day 2: Architecture, Art, and Alvar Aalto

MORNING: **HELSINKI CATHEDRAL & SENATE SQUARE**

Explore the neoclassical heart of Helsinki, with its iconic white cathedral and surrounding monumental buildings.

LUNCH: **KAPPELI**

Dine in a historic glass pavilion, offering traditional dishes amidst a backdrop of Esplanadi Park.

AFTERNOON: **ATENEUM ART MUSEUM**

Dive into Finnish art, from classics to contemporary. Don't miss works inspired by the Kalevala, the Finnish national epic.

EVENING: **KUURNA**

Tucked away in Kruununhaka, this restaurant brings modern twists to traditional dishes.

Day 3: Nature, Nooks, and Nordic Tales

MORNING: CENTRAL LIBRARY OODI

Beyond books, this architectural marvel offers workshops, a cinema, and terraces with city views.

LUNCH: FLEURISTE

A chic French café in Ullanlinna, perfect for quiches and pastries.

AFTERNOON: SEURASAARI OPEN-AIR MUSEUM

Step back in time in this forested island, showcasing traditional Finnish wooden buildings.

EVENING: TISLAAMO DISTILLERY BAR

End your journey with craft spirits in this local distillery.

From its design-forward cityscape to its deep-rooted traditions, Helsinki offers a balanced brew of the old and the new. As you leave, carry with you a piece of its serene Nordic spirit and perhaps a Moomin or two!

St. Petersburg

Palaces, Paintings, and Pierogi

Day 1: Palaces, Plazas, and Plenty of Gold

MORNING: **The Hermitage/Winter Palace**

Dive into one of the world's largest art collections. Try not to get lost, but if you do, may it be between a Rembrandt and a Picasso.

LUNCH: **Stolle**

Pies, pies, and more pies. Sweet or savory, this is the place to get a real taste of Russian baking.

AFTERNOON: **Peter and Paul Fortress**

Explore the birthplace of St. Petersburg. Pro tip: Time your visit for the noon cannon shot. SPOILER: It's loud.

EVENING: **Mariinsky Theatre**

Experience a ballet or opera in this historic theater. Keep an eye out for ghosts of prima ballerinas past!

Character of the City:

Where Europe meets Russia with a dramatic flourish, St. Petersburg is a dance of tsarist grandeur, world-class art, and canals that could make Venice a tad jealous. Plus, it's the only city where it's perfectly acceptable to daydream about being an 18th-century aristocrat in the morning and a modern-day foodie by evening.

Day 2: Cathedrals, Canals, and Caviar Dreams

MORNING: Church of the Savior on Spilled Blood

With a name that's almost as long as its history, this mosaic wonder is a must-visit.

LUNCH: Gogol

A nod to the famous Russian writer, feast on traditional dishes in a cozy ambiance.

AFTERNOON: Canal Cruise

Glide through St. Petersburg's waterways and soak in the architecture from a duck's perspective.

EVENING:

Russian Vodka Room No.1

Taste (responsibly) a plethora of vodkas and ponder why you haven't been sipping this elixir all your life.

Day 3: Estates, Exhibits, and Evening Enchantments

MORNING: Peterhof Palace

Marvel at Russia's answer to Versailles. Spoiler: there will
be fountains. Many, many fountains.

LUNCH: Katyusha

njoy hearty Russian fare with a view of the Nevsky Prospekt.
Who said borscht was boring?

AFTERNOON: Faberge Museum

Revel in the opulence of the famous Fabergé eggs. No, they don't
contain chocolate.

EVENING: Belmond Grand Hotel Europe

Jazz, history, and sumptuous dining converge here. Even if you
don't stay, it's worth a visit.

As you bid "до свидания" (goodbye) to this Russian gem, may your
heart be lighter, your art knowledge deeper, and your suitcase...
perhaps bursting with nesting dolls! 🏰🖼️🪆🇷🇺

Zagreb's Charm

Quaint Trams, Sartorial Roots, and Dragon Lore OVER A WEEKEND

Day 1: Statues, Strolls, and Some Unusual Art

MORNING: BAN JELACIC SQUARE

Kick off in the heart of Zagreb. Rumor has it that if you don't start here, you haven't really seen Zagreb.

LUNCH: BALTAZAR

Enjoy grilled dishes as you ponder why dragons aren't the city's official mascot.

AFTERNOON:

MUSEUM OF BROKEN RELATIONSHIPS

Ever kept that teddy bear from your ex? So did others, and they made a museum about it. Therapeutic and oddly fascinating!

EVENING: TKALCICEVA STREET

A former river now flooded with cafes, bars, and the echoes of 1,000 heart-to-heart chats.

CHARACTER OF THE CITY:

Ah, Zagreb! Where Central Europe, the Mediterranean, and the Balkans playfully collide. It's a city of rooftop vistas, quirky museums, and coffee that demands you to slow down and enjoy. And if you thought ties were just a boring office attire, think again. Zagreb's about to school you in sartorial history!

Day 2: Towers, Ties, and Tram Tales

MORNING: Lotrscak Tower

A cannon fires from here daily at noon. Because why not? It's a timeless alarm clock (pun intended).

LUNCH: Agava

Savor Croatian cuisine with a twist, wondering if the tie (or as locals call it, "cravat") you're wearing was indeed a Croatian invention. Spoiler: It was!

AFTERNOON: Zagreb's Funicular

It's one of the world's shortest, but it'll elevate your spirits in no time!

EVENING: Vinodol

Indulge in traditional fare and toast to the inventiveness of a city that turned neckties into an international fashion statement.

Day 3: Markets, Museums, and Maksimir Delights

MORNING: Dolac Market

Rub elbows with locals, sample cheeses, and perhaps snag a dragon-themed souvenir. Every city has its myths!

LUNCH: Mali Bar

Delight in inventive dishes as you reflect on how this city has stealthily stolen your heart.

AFTERNOON: Maksimir Park & Zoo

Stroll in the oldest Southeast European public park. Keep an eye out for 4D chess players and birds that might've inspired Twitter.

EVENING: Dezman Bar

Wind down with cocktails that could make James Bond swap his martini preferences.

As you wave goodbye to Zagreb, may your heart be filled with joy, your pockets with quirky souvenirs, and your tie game be forever strong!

Porto

Bridges, Barrels, and a Bounty of Bacalhau

Day 1: Riverfront Reveries and Riverside Toasts

MORNING: LIVRARIA LELLO

Begin your journey in one of the world's most stunning bookstores. Rumor has it J.K. Rowling got a smidge of inspiration here for a certain magical series. No biggie.

LUNCH: CANTINA 32

Dive into Portuguese flavors. And yes, bacalhau (salt cod) will likely be on the menu. It's like the Beyoncé of Portuguese cuisine.

AFTERNOON: RIBEIRA DISTRICT

Wander the historic heart of Porto. Cobbled streets? Check. Colorful houses? Check. Irresistible charm? Double check.

CHARACTER OF THE CITY:

Ahhh, Porto. The city where the Douro River gleams, the wine flows endlessly, and the alleys whisper tales of seafarers. If Lisbon is Portugal's glamorous sibling, Porto is the cool, artsy one, with tattoos of historic landmarks and a soundtrack of Fado tunes.

EVENING: WINE QUAY BAR

Sip on vinho verde as you gaze out at the Douro. Feel poetic? That's the Porto effect.

Day 2: Bridges, Bargains, and Bacalhau (again)

MORNING: DOM LUIS I BRIDGE

A double-deck iron bridge with views that'll
make your Instagram followers green with envy.

LUNCH: MERCADO DO BOLHAO

Dive into the bustling market. Grab some cheese, olives, and yes, perhaps
more bacalhau. One can never have enough!

AFTERNOON: SERRALVES MUSEUM AND GARDENS

Contemporary art meets manicured gardens. If Porto had a dating
profile, this would be its lead photo.

EVENING:

MAJESTIC CAFE

Step back in time in this historic café.
It's like Downton Abbey, but with more
pastries and less drama.

Day 3: Cellars, Churches, and Culinary Delights

MORNING: CLERIGOS TOWER

Climb for panoramic city views. But maybe after that third pastel de nata wasn't a good idea.

LUNCH: ADEGA SAO NICOLAU

Embrace traditional dishes in a rustic setting. Did someone say bacalhau? Oh, yes. We're going for a hat trick.

AFTERNOON: PORT WINE CELLARS

Learn and taste the magic of Port wine. And perhaps wonder why you haven't moved to Porto yet.

EVENING: CASA DE LO

Round off with Fado music and a glass (or three) of Port. Because in Porto, the night isn't complete without some soulful tunes.

As you bid "adeus" to Porto, may your heart feel richer, your palate more refined, and your suitcase... slightly heavier with wine bottles. Cheers to the city that ages as gracefully as its barrels! 🍷🏰🎶⏺

Granada

Alhambra Dreams, Tapas Tales, and Flamenco Flares

Day 1: Palaces, Plazas, and Passionate Performances

MORNING: Alhambra

Begin at the legendary Alhambra. Once home to sultans and their secrets, now it's your turn to be mesmerized. Pro tip: Whispering sweet nothings to the ancient walls might not reveal its secrets, but it'll make for a great Instagram story!

LUNCH: Calle Navas

Head downtown to the renowned tapas street, Calle Navas. Remember, in Granada, ordering a drink means you'll get a free tapa. It's like Happy Hour, but all day. Buen provecho!

AFTERNOON: Albaicín

Time to get lost! Wander through the labyrinthine streets of the Albaicín, the old Moorish quarter. Each corner promises a new view, a hidden plaza, or a chatty cat ready to share the local gossip.

EVENING: Sacromonte

As the sun dips, head to the Sacromonte caves for a passionate flamenco performance. The fervor of the dancers, the rhythm of the guitars, and the clapping hands will make you want to shout, "¡Olé!" Just make sure you don't spill your sangria.

> ### CHARACTER OF THE CITY:
> Hola from Granada! A city where Moorish history dances cheek to cheek with modern Spanish flair. Nestled at the foot of the Sierra Nevada mountains, Granada beckons with tales of sultans, flamenco, and – not to forget – free tapas!

Day 2: Baths, Bites, and Breathtaking Views

MORNING: ROYAL CHAPEL OF GRANADA

Mingle with the royals – or at least their resting places. Pay your respects to the Catholic Monarchs, Isabel and Ferdinand. (No, they don't rise and dance, even if you ask politely.)

LUNCH: PLAZA BIB-RAMBLA

This bustling square is chock-full of eateries. Grab a table, and let the parade of people-watching begin. Remember to try "piononos," the sweet little treats that are the pride of nearby Santa Fe.

AFTERNOON: HAMMAM AL ANDALUS

Take a dip in Granada's Arabian-style baths. These aren't your average puddles, mind you. With soothing music and aromatic scents, you'll emerge more relaxed than a cat in a sunbeam.

EVENING: MIRADOR DE SAN NICOLAS

As twilight approaches, join locals and tourists alike at this famous viewpoint. The Alhambra against the backdrop of the Sierra Nevada is pure magic. No, seriously, we think they sprinkle it with pixie dust.

Day 3: Guitars, Gardens, and Gobble-worthy Churros

MORNING: GENERALIFE GARDENS

These are the gardens the sultans chilled in. Exotic plants, fountains that might make you contemplate a career in poetry, and views that scream "This is why you travel!"

LUNCH: EL HUERTO DE JUAN RANAS

A feast for your stomach and eyes. Eat with the Alhambra peeping over your shoulder. Try not to blush.

AFTERNOON: CARRERA DEL DARRO

Labeled one of the most beautiful streets in Spain, it's a stroll down history lane. With ancient bridges and the Darro River whispering tales, you'll wonder if you've stepped into a Cervantes novel.

EVENING: CHURRERIA ALHAMBRA

End your whirlwind Granada trip with churros dipped in chocolate. Crunchy, warm, and just the right amount of messy. A sweet ending to a delicious adventure!

Granada in 72 hours? You did it! And while we couldn't fit in every nook and cranny, we promise you've gotten a delightful taste. Until next time, travelers. Keep your passport handy and your sense of humor ready!

TRĪS BRĀĻI

RIGA

11.NOVEMBRA KRASTMALA

1
6
4
6

VE

Riga Reverie

Nouveau Splendor, Historic Timber, and a Toast with BALZAMS IN THREE DAYS

DAY 1: Cobblestones, Chronicles, and Creamy Cakes

MORNING: **Riga's Old Town**

Kick off your journey in the UNESCO-listed heart of Riga. Wander around winding streets and open squares, but watch out for those cheeky cobblestones; they've been tripping tourists for centuries!

LUNCH: **Riga Central Market**

Housed in former Zeppelin hangars (yes, you read that right!), it's Europe's largest market and bazaar. Dive into local delicacies. Pickled herring, anyone?

CHARACTER OF THE CITY:

Welcome to Riga! This Latvian gem is where centuries-old timbered houses stand proudly next to Art Nouveau masterpieces. With a history as rich as its Black Balsam liquor, Riga is ready to serve up a weekend full of surprises!

AFTERNOON: **House of the Blackheads**

Marvel at this architectural wonder and its deep-rooted history. Legend has it, if you squint hard enough, you can see the footprints of the merchants who once danced here.

EVENING: **Folkklubs ALA Pagrabs**

Experience Latvia's vibrant folk culture with live music, traditional dances, and plenty of local brew. Don't know the steps? Just follow the lead of the spirited locals!

Day 2: Spirals, Stories, and Sips

MORNING: **Art Nouveau District**

Put on your fanciest walking shoes and strut through the streets that showcase some of the finest Art Nouveau buildings in Europe. Remember, it's all in the details!

LUNCH: **Lido**

Dig into hearty Latvian dishes in this iconic eatery. Warning: The potato pancakes have been known to inspire spontaneous song and dance.

AFTERNOON: **The Freedom Monument**

Pay your respects at this symbol of Latvia's independence and resilience. It's also a favorite spot for pigeon-watching, but we can't promise they'll pose for your photos.

EVENING: **Skyline Bar**

Elevate your evening at this trendy bar. With panoramic views of the city, sip on cocktails and let Riga's skyline dazzle you.

Day 3: Timber, Towers, and Toasty Saunas

MORNING: Ethnographic Open-Air Museum

Journey back in time and explore traditional Latvian rural life. If you're lucky, you might just get invited to a centuries-old tea party.

LUNCH: Kalku Varti

Nestled in the heart of Old Town, treat yourself to gourmet Latvian cuisine. The beetroot soup is a symphony in a bowl!

AFTERNOON: Riga Cathedral

Climb the tower and bask in a bird's-eye view of Riga. Just remember, what goes up must come down!

EVENING: Latvian Sauna Ritual

Wind down your Riga adventure with an authentic sauna experience. Steam, herbs, and gentle whisks of the birch branch will leave you rejuvenated and ready for your next adventure.

Wrap Up:

Three days in Riga? Checked off! As you leave this Baltic beauty, take a piece of it with you — be it a memory, a souvenir, or a mysterious stain from that adventurous dinner. Farewell, dear traveler! Until our next escapade!

Warsaw

Mermaids, Mazurkas, and Milk Bars in 72 Hours

Day 1: Legends, Lazienki, and Luscious Bites

MORNING: Royal Castle

Delve deep into Poland's regal history at this meticulously reconstructed palace. Rumor has it the echoing chambers sometimes whisper tales from centuries ago. (Ear trumpet not included.)

LUNCH: Milk Bar (Bar Mleczny)

Experience a trip down memory lane in these socialist-era eateries. The pierogi here might just steal your heart... and your appetite.

AFTERNOON: Lazienki Park

Stroll amidst regal peacocks, grand statues, and the stunning Palace on the Isle. If you're lucky, you might stumble upon a Chopin piano concert in the open air. Ah, the melodies!

CHARACTER OF THE CITY:

Step into Warsaw, Poland's resilient phoenix, a city that rose from the ashes of its turbulent past to proudly flaunt a fusion of the old and the modern. With legends of mermaids, a fondness for pierogi, and music that tugs at your heartstrings, Warsaw invites you for a rollercoaster of discovery!

EVENING: Nowy Swiat Street

As the city lights twinkle, meander down one of Warsaw's liveliest streets, home to quaint cafes, boutiques, and street musicians strumming nostalgic tunes.

Day 2: Uprisings, Unicorns, and Underground Joints

MORNING: **WARSAW UPRISING MUSEUM**

Dive into the soul of Warsaw and its spirited resistance during WWII. A place of profound stories and unsung heroes.

LUNCH: **HALA KOSZYKI**

Warsaw's trendy food hall. From Polish kielbasa to vegan delights, there's something to tickle every taste bud.

AFTERNOON: **WILANOW PALACE**

Dubbed the "Polish Versailles", roam the ornate chambers and lush gardens, and wonder why your own home feels suddenly under-decorated.

EVENING:

PAWILONY

Tucked behind Nowy Swiat, discover a warren of tiny bars. Quirky, cozy, and oh-so-Warsaw. Try a shot of Żubrówka (bison grass vodka)

IF YOU'RE
FEELING BRAVE!

Day 3: Mermaids, Mazurkas, and Modern Art

MORNING: Old Town and Mermaid Statue

Wander the cobblestoned streets and square, then pay respects to the city's beloved mermaid, defender of Warsaw. Selfies encouraged.

LUNCH: Zapiecek

Dive fork-first into traditional Polish fare. More pierogi, please!

AFTERNOON: Copernicus Science Center

Unleash your inner Einstein in this hands-on science playground. Perfect for both kids and adults who refuse to grow up.

EVENING: Praga District

Cross the river to this gritty-turned-arty district. Explore alternative galleries, sip on craft brews, and sway to the beats of underground music venues.

Warsaw in 72 hours? Mission accomplished! As you bid "Do widzenia" to this dynamic city, remember the tales, the tastes, and the toe-tapping tunes. Adventure awaits in every corner of the world, and I'm here to guide you through them all. Safe travels!

Luxembourg City

Castles, Cuisines, and Cobblestone Charms in a Weekend Escape

Day 1: Palaces, Promenades, and Perfect Pastries

MORNING: Grand Ducal Palace

Dive into regal luxury. Wave like you own the place and pretend to be a royal for a minute. After all, it's vacation time.

LUNCH: Chocolate House by Nathalie Bonn

A stone's throw from the palace, indulge in sweet and savory treats. The hot chocolate here? It's like a hug in a cup.

AFTERNOON: Chemins de la Corniche

Dubbed the most beautiful balcony in Europe. A walk here promises panoramic views and oodles of photo ops.

EVENING: Grund

Descend into this picturesque district by the Alzette River. With fairy-lit streets and charming taverns, it feels like time decided to take a nap here.

CHARACTER OF THE CITY:

Enter Luxembourg City, a pocket-sized powerhouse brimming with multi-layered history, grand ducal tales, and valleys that seem to have sprung straight from a storybook. It's where modern finance flirts with medieval charm, and every cobblestone seems to have its own secret to tell.

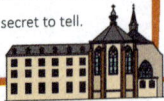

Day 2: Forts, Fables, and Flavorful Feasts

MORNING: Bock Casemates

Explore the vast underground tunnels that once shielded the city. Tip: Echoing your name is fun, but remember, those walls have ears!

LUNCH: Mousel's Cantine

Savor traditional dishes like 'Gromperekichelcher'. It's a mouthful to say but even more of a delight to eat.

AFTERNOON: Villa Vauban

Dive into art from the 18th and 19th centuries. Contemplating a painting might not give you the artist's original intent, but it will grant you bragging rights.

EVENING: Am Tirmschen

Nestled in a historic building, enjoy a cozy dinner. A side of fondue with a splash of Luxembourgish wine? Heavenly!

Day 3: Markets, Museums, and Midnight Toasts

MORNING: Place Guillaume II

Whether it's a bustling market or an open-air concert, there's always something afoot at this lively square.

LUNCH: Kniddelen at De Gudde Wellen

Dive into this traditional dumpling dish. Top it off with apple cider and thank me later.

AFTERNOON: Mudam

Contemporary art galore! Interact, interpret, and maybe even impersonate – after all, art is subjective!

EVENING: Urban Bar & Kitchen

Raise a toast to your fabulous Luxembourg City escapade. Sip, savor, and reminisce.

Three delightful days in Luxembourg City? Done and dusted! As you head home, clutching souvenirs and memories, remember: there's a whole world out there, and every city has a tale to tell. Keep exploring, intrepid traveler! 🌍✨

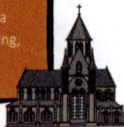

Ljubljana

Dragons, Decaf, and Dreamy Bridges

Day 1: Dragons, Daydreams, and Delicious Bites

MORNING: LJUBLJANA CASLE

Ride the funicular or flex those calves up the hill to this medieval marvel. The view from the top? It's like Ljubljana decided to pose just for you.

LUNCH:

OPEN KITCHEN (ODPRTA KUHNA)

If it's a Friday, you're in luck! Experience Slovenia's best culinary offerings all in one bustling marketplace.

CHARACTER OF THE CITY:

Behold Ljubljana, the whimsical Slovenian capital, where legends of dragons mingle with a laid-back café culture and winding river tales. This is where green spaces whisper ancient stories, and bridges aren't just crossings but canvases of culture.

AFTERNOON: DRAGON BRIDGE

Snap a selfie with the iconic dragons. Legend says they wag their tails when a virgin crosses the bridge. (No pressure!)

EVENING: METELKOVA

Wander through this autonomous cultural zone, a splash of graffiti, art installations, and alternative vibes. It's like Ljubljana's edgy younger sibling.

Day 2: Canals, Cafés, and Cobblestone Chronicles

MORNING: BOAT RIDE ON THE LJUBLJANICA RIVER

Glide and admire the city's stunning architecture from a
duck's viewpoint. Quacking optional.

LUNCH: COMPA

Dive into traditional Slovenian dishes. Try the "štruklji" - it's
a roll of deliciousness, literally.

AFTERNOON: TIVOLI PARK

Ljubljana's green lung. Perfect for a lazy stroll, picnics, or
just befriending local squirrels.

EVENING: LJUBLJANA'S RIVERSIDE CAFES

Pick a spot, grab a local wine or decaf
(they love it!), and soak in the ambiance.

Day 3: Markets, Museums, and Melodic Evenings

MORNING: **Central Market**

Rub shoulders with locals. Fresh produce, fragrant herbs, and the occasional grandparent's secret recipe await.

LUNCH: **Gostilna Na Gradu**

A gastronomic haven set within the castle walls. A blend of tradition and modernity on your plate.

AFTERNOON: **National Gallery**

Immerse yourself in Slovenia's rich artistic tapestry. Each brushstroke tells a tale.

EVENING: **Orto Bar**

Groove to live music. From rock to reggae, there's a beat for every soul.

Three enchanting days in Ljubljana? Mission accomplished! As you bid "Nasvidenje" to the dragon city, remember the magic, the melodies, and the moments. Ready for another adventure? Just say the word. Safe travels, wanderer! 🐉✨🍷

Belgrade Vibes

Fortress Views, Bohemian Rhythms, and A Weekend of Balkan Energy

Day 1: Fortresses, Floating Rafts, and Fabulous Feasts

MORNING: Kalemegdan Fortress

Start with a deep dive into Belgrade's storied past at this iconic fortress. The panoramic views? They might just make you want to pen an ode to the city.

LUNCH: Manufaktura

Treat yourself to Serbian culinary wonders. The ajvar and kajmak are non-negotiables!

AFTERNOON: Knez Mihailova Street

Window shop and people-watch along this bustling pedestrian boulevard, the city's main artery of art, culture, and commerce.

CHARACTER OF THE CITY:

Embark on a journey through Belgrade, the Serbian capital where tales of empires past coalesce with urban cool. This city, perched at the confluence of the Sava and Danube rivers, is where resilient spirit dances to pulsating nightlife and where every cobblestone echoes history and hedonism.

EVENING: Splavovi

Experience Belgrade's famed floating nightclubs and bars on the rivers. Here, the Balkan beats will make sure your feet have a mind of their own.

Day 2: Bohemian Rhapsodies, Brutalism, and Bistros

MORNING: Skadarlija

Traverse the bohemian heart of Belgrade. Cobblestones, kafanas (traditional taverns), and poetic vibes are the order of the day.

LUNCH: Dva Jelena

A staple in Skadarlija. Revel in the taste of traditional dishes, serenaded by live tamburica bands.

AFTERNOON: Yugoslav History Museum and House of Flowers

Explore Yugoslavia's complex past and pay a visit to Tito's mausoleum.

EVENING: BETONSKA GALERIJA

A stretch of urban street art. It's like Belgrade's diary written in splashes of color and creativity.

Day 3: Markets, Museums, and Melancholic Tunes

MORNING: ZEMUN

Wander this picturesque part of the city, marked by its Austro-Hungarian architecture. Don't forget to climb the Gardos Tower for another spellbinding view.

LUNCH: BAHUS

Situated in Zemun, dive into a plate of sarma and let the flavors narrate tales of old.

AFTERNOON: NIKOLA TESLA MUSEUM

Get electrified (not literally!) by the life and works of this genius inventor.

EVENING: KLUB 20/44

Conclude your trip swaying to an eclectic mix of music on this legendary boat club. It's as if the entire city's energy converges here.

Three dazzling days in Belgrade? Done! As you bid "Dovidenja" to Serbia's soulful capital, carry with you the rhythms, the relics, and the rhapsodies. Ready for your next escapade? I'm here to spin the tale. Happy voyaging! 🌆🎶🎻

Sofia Sojourn

Ancient Sanctuaries, Serene Spaces, and a Weekend of Bulgarian Harmony

Day 1: Domes, Delights, and Downtown Beats

MORNING: Alexander Nevsky Cathedral

Commence your day beneath the gleaming domes of this Neo-Byzantine masterpiece. Its beauty is rivaled only by its history.

LUNCH: Happy Bar & Grill

Dive into Bulgarian flavors with a modern twist. Kavarma, a meaty treat, is a must-try!

AFTERNOON: Vitosha Boulevard

Shop, stroll, and sip along Sofia's most famous street. You might just spot a pop-up performance or two.

CHARACTER OF THE CITY:

Step into Sofia, Bulgaria's age-old capital, where the shadows of Thracians, Romans, and Byzantines gracefully waltz with contemporary vibes. Nestled at the foot of Vitosha Mountain, Sofia is a medley of golden domes, verdant parks, and tales as old as time.

EVENING: Rakia & Co

Experience Bulgaria's iconic spirit, rakia, in this trendy spot. But beware: this drink has a kick as strong as a Bulgarian folk dance!

Day 2: Museums, Markets, and Mountain Views

MORNING: National Museum of History

Time-travel through Bulgaria's epochs, from ancient gold treasures to modern memorabilia.

LUNCH: Made in Home

A haven for organic and artisanal Bulgarian dishes. The banitsa here whispers tales of grandmothers' kitchens.

AFTERNOON: Vitosha Mountain

Just a stone's throw from the city, rejuvenate amidst nature. Opt for a light trek or simply bask in the panoramic vistas.

EVENING: One More Bar

Relax in this cozy retro setting, sipping cocktails inspired by old Sofia.

Day 3: Ruins, Rotundas, and Rhythmic Nights

MORNING: SERDIKA'S ANCIENT COMPLEX

Traverse the ancient Roman ruins right in the heart of Sofia. History underfoot at every step!

LUNCH: THE LITTLE THINGS

Indulge in gourmet delights that blend Bulgarian tradition with international flair.

AFTERNOON: ROTUNDA OF ST. GEORGE

Marvel at Sofia's oldest preserved building, where layers of history unfold in beautiful frescoes.

EVENING: SWINGIN' HALL

Wrap up your trip grooving to live jazz tunes, feeling the city's heartbeat sync with the rhythms.

Three soulful days in Sofia? Check! As you bid "Довиждане" (Dovizhdane) to this Balkan beauty, cherish the sanctuaries, the stories, and the serenades. When wanderlust strikes again, I'm here, ready to guide. Safe travels, globetrotter! 🌍🏛️🎷

Tallinn

Towers, Tales, and Time-Honored Traditions

Day 1: Turrets, Treasures, and Twilight Tipples

MORNING: **Toompea Castle**

Begin atop Tallinn's hill in this ancient stronghold. The view? It's as if the city unfurls a tapestry of history before your very eyes.

LUNCH: **Rataskaevu 16**

Savor Estonian cuisine in a charming setting. The beetroot soup tells tales of time-honored recipes.

AFTERNOON: **Tallinn Old Town**

Amble through Europe's best-preserved medieval city. Every stone and spire has a saga to share.

EVENING: **III Draakon**

Step into this candlelit tavern for hearty pies and honey beer, served with a side of medieval merriment.

CHARACTER OF THE CITY:

Journey into Tallinn, where medieval splendor mingles effortlessly with digital dynamism. Estonia's capital, perched on the Baltic shores, is a blend of ancient spires, cobbled lanes, and cyber cafes. Here, fairy tales aren't just stories; they're your daily itinerary.

Day 2: Museums, Markets, and Melodic Moments

MORNING: Kumu Art Museum

Delve into Estonia's artistic soul in this stunning modern structure.

LUNCH: F-Hoone

Located in the trendy Telliskivi area, this spot offers modern twists on Estonian classics.

AFTERNOON: Seaplane Harbour (Lennusadam)

Explore this maritime museum, featuring ships, submarines, and stories of the sea.

EVENING: Clayhills Gastropub

Immerse yourself in live music sessions, absorbing the rhythms of Tallinn's contemporary scene.

Day 3: Churches, Chocolates, and Cobblestone Chronicles

MORNING: St. Olaf's Church

Climb the spiraling steps. At the pinnacle, Tallinn lies beneath,
like a mosaic of memories.

LUNCH: Kalev Chocolate Shop

Not a conventional lunch spot, but who can resist a
chocolate-making workshop and sampling session?

AFTERNOON: Kadriorg Palace and Park

Meander through this Tsarist-era palace and its lush gardens. It's a
brushstroke of Russian romance in an Estonian epic.

EVENING: NOA Chef's Hall

Conclude your journey with a gourmet meal, overlooking the Baltic.
Each bite is a crescendo of your Tallinn tale.

Three days among Tallinn's turrets and tales? Mission splendidly
accomplished! As you bid "Hüvasti" to this Baltic gem, let the towers,
traditions, and tunes linger in your heart. Whenever the travel bug bites
next, I'm here to craft your adventure. Fare thee well, traveler! 🏰🌅

Seville Serenade

Echoes of Flamenco, Moorish Majesty, in the Vibrant Pulse of ANDALUSIA

Day 1: Cathedrals, Courtyards, and Churros Con Chocolate

MORNING: Seville Cathedral & La Giralda

The world's largest Gothic cathedral beckons. Climbing the Giralda bell tower? Mandatory for panoramic views and instant Instagram fame.

LUNCH: El Rinconcillo

Seville's oldest bar, dating back to 1670. The tapas here are as timeless as the tiled walls.

AFTERNOON: Real Alcazar

Dive into a mosaic of Christian and Moorish architecture. The gardens? Straight out of a sultan's dream.

> **CHARACTER OF THE CITY:**
>
> Seville is passion personified. From its torrid history of Moors and monarchs to the seductive dance of flamenco, the city sways with stories and sizzles in the Andalusian sun. Seville whispers old tales through its cobbled streets and shouts its culture from every rooftop terrace.

EVENING: Tablao El Arenal

Witness the fiery passion of flamenco. Your feet might involuntarily tap along. Don't resist.

Day 2: Plazas, Palaces, and Plenty of Jamón

MORNING: Plaza de Espana

A Renaissance-Moorish dream. Take a boat ride in the canal, and you might feel like a Spanish prince/princess for a moment.

LUNCH: Mercado de Triana

Over the Triana Bridge lies a market bursting with flavors. The jamón ibérico? It's a love story in every bite.

AFTERNOON: Casa de Pilatos

A lesser-known palace with a blend of architectural styles. It's like history's own sampler platter

EVENING: Calle Betis

Metropol Parasol (Las Setas)

This wooden structure offers city views at sunset. The nickname means "The Mushrooms." Fungi have never looked this chic.

Day 3: Barrios, Boats, and Bravado-filled Evenings

MORNING: Barrio Santa Cruz

Lose yourself in Seville's historic Jewish quarter. Every alley has a tale, every square, a secret.

LUNCH: Bodega Santa Cruz (Las Columnas)

Another iconic tapas spot. Maybe try the salmorejo, a cold tomato soup that's the essence of summer.

AFTERNOON: Guadalquivir River Cruise

Sail the historic river. If you squint, you might see explorers of old setting sail to the New World.

EVENING: Calle Betis

A riverside stretch with bars and zest for life. As the sun sets, Seville's spirit truly shines here.

Three days in Seville, and you've tasted history, danced with duende (the spirit of flamenco), and likely pondered a permanent move to Andalusia. Hasta luego! And remember, Seville not only stays in the heart but also rhythmically beats within it. 🎺⚫🎸

Valencia

A Weekend of Color, Hills, and Delicious Paellas

Day 1: Cathedrals, Courtyards, and Culinary Conquests

MORNING: Valencia Cathedral

Begin amidst Gothic, Baroque, and Romanesque glories.
Rumor has it, the Holy Grail resides here. Ready for the quest?

LUNCH: Central Market

Amongst the art-nouveau splendors, dig into
local tapas. Don't forget to sip on the
delightful horchata!

AFTERNOON: La Lonja de la Seda

Marvel at this UNESCO-listed silk
exchange, where architectural elegance
weaves tales of a merchant past.

CHARACTER OF THE CITY:

Plunge into Valencia, where the
old-world charm meets futuristic
marvels. Spain's third-largest city is a
sun-drenched delight where oranges
sweeten the air, Gothic grandeur
meets space-age splendors, and
where the sea kisses golden sands.

EVENING: Barrio del Carmen

As twilight descends, wander this ancient
district's alleys, before settling in a local
taverna for wines and whims.

Day 2: Futurism, Festivals, and Flavorful Feasts

MORNING: CITY OF ARTS AND SCIENCES

Dive into Valencia's modern side. From an opera house to a planetarium, it's like strolling in a sci-fi novella.

LUNCH: CASA ROBERTO

For an authentic Valencian paella, this is your stop. Each bite promises sun, sea, and Spanish secrets.

AFTERNOON: MUSEO FALLERO

Dive deep into the traditions of Valencia's famed Fallas festival. Fiery festivity, anyone?

EVENING: MARINA BEACH CLUB

Feel the Mediterranean breeze as you sip cocktails and groove to beats under a canopy of stars.

Day 3: Gardens, Galleries, and Gastronomic Goodness

MORNING: Turia Gardens

Where a river once flowed, now lies a verdant vein of
Valencia. Perfect for a leisurely cycle or stroll.

LUNCH: La Pepica

A beachside treat! Savor fresh seafood paella, gazing at waves
dancing to flamenco rhythms.

AFTERNOON: Institut Valencia d'Art Modern (IVAM)

Immerse in Valencia's contemporary art scene.
Creativity and color converge here.

EVENING: Ruzafa District

Valencia's hipster heart. Eclectic bars, quirky boutiques,
and a finale of delicious tapas to wrap your journey.

Three sun-soaked days in Valencia? Exquisitely enjoyed! As you whisper
"Adiós" to this Mediterranean marvel, let the paellas, plazas, and
palaces play in your memories. And when wanderlust beckons afresh,
just summon me. Safe and savory voyages ahead! 🍷🍽✈

Geneva

A Weekend of Glaciers, Grandeur, and Gourmet Gouda

Day 1: Lakes, Landmarks, and Luscious Fondue

MORNING: Jet d'Eau

Initiate your Geneva journey with this iconic water fountain, shooting majestically from the lake's serene surface.

LUNCH: Cafe du Centre

Delight in traditional Swiss fare. A cheesy raclette? Yes, please!

AFTERNOON: St. Pierre Cathedral

Ascend the towers of this historical edifice. Geneva unfurls beneath you, a tapestry of tales and tiles.

CHARACTER OF THE CITY:

Dive into Geneva, where pristine Alpine breezes meet international intrigue. Nestled on the shores of Lake Geneva (or Lac Léman to locals), this Swiss sensation is a symphony of diplomacy, precision, and chocolate-dipped elegance.

EVENING: Carouge

Stroll in this bohemian district, absorbing Italianate charm and perhaps pausing at a wine bar for a flute of local white.

Day 2: Museums, Markets, and Molten Chocolate

MORNING: Palais des Nations

As Europe's UN hub, this place buzzes with diplomacy. Tour the chambers, gardens, and perhaps dream up a peace treaty or two.

LUNCH: Les Armures

When in Geneva, fondue is mandatory! Dip into molten goodness in this historic setting.

AFTERNOON: Patek Philippe Museum

Revel in Swiss precision, exploring the world of haute horlogerie. Those ticking masterpieces aren't just watches; they're art.

EVENING: English Garden

Lounge by the luminous L'Horloge Fleurie (Flower Clock) and let Lake Geneva's shimmer serenade you.

Day 3: Boats, Boutiques, and Breathtaking Views

MORNING: Lake Geneva Cruise

Glide over crystalline waters, with the Alps nodding in approval from the horizon.

LUNCH: Cottage Cafe

Amidst verdant tranquility, savor light bites, dreaming of Alpine adventures and diplomatic dances.

AFTERNOON: Rue du Rhone

Indulge in retail therapy, Geneva-style. From luxury boutiques to chocolatiers, there's a Swiss souvenir awaiting every taste.

EVENING: L'Atelier Cocktail Club

Conclude with handcrafted cocktails, as Geneva's lights twinkle in sync with your spirited sips.

Three days amidst Geneva's grace? Magnificently managed! As you bid "Au Revoir" to this lakeside luminary, may the memories of glaciers, grand halls, and gourmet delights glide in your mind. And whenever the winds of wanderlust whisper again, here I am. Onward to the next adventure, explorer! 🏔️🍫🍷

Milan

Maestros, Moda, and Moreish Milanese IN 72 HOURS

Day 1: Duomos, Districts, and Delectable Dining

MORNING: Milan Cathedral (Duomo di Milano)

Start grand, beneath the spires of this iconic cathedral. If your fitness permits, ascend to the rooftop for a breathtaking panorama.

LUNCH: Luini

Just a hop away from the Duomo, treat yourself to a legendary panzerotti. It's like a pizza pocket of joy!

CHARACTER OF THE CITY:

Stride into Milan, Italy's pulsating heart of fashion, finance, and fabulousness. With its Gothic grandeur juxtaposed against modern minimalist marvels, Milan is where Da Vinci's musings dance with dapper designers, all under the Mediterranean sun.

AFTERNOON: Galleria Vittorio Emanuele II

Marvel at the world's oldest active shopping mall. Label lovers, prepare your wallets!

EVENING: Brera District

Wander through cobbled streets, soaking in bohemian vibes and perhaps pausing for an aperitivo or two.

Day 2: Artistry, Avenues, and Authentic Aperitifs

MORNING: SANTA MARIA DELLE GRAZIE

A date with Da Vinci awaits! Gaze upon "The Last Supper" and absorb the genius.

LUNCH: TRATTORIA MILANESE

Embrace traditional Milan with a plate of osso buco or risotto alla Milanese.

AFTERNOON: SFORZA CASTLE

Explore this historic fortress turned museum, surrounded by serene parks and fountains.

EVENING:

NAVIGLI DISTRICT

Reflect by the canals, enjoying the tapestry of boutiques, galleries, and eateries. An evening gelato here? Essential.

Day 3: Modernity, Museums, and Milanese Magic

MORNING: Bosco Verticale

Revel in Milan's contemporary side by visiting these vertical forests. Green architecture at its finest!

LUNCH: Eataly

An ode to Italy's culinary wonders, pick from a smorgasbord of regional delicacies.

AFTERNOON: Pinacoteca di Brera

Dive into an art sanctuary, housing works from the likes of Raphael, Caravaggio, and Bellini.

EVENING: Corso Como 10

Conclude in this eclectic space – part bookstore, gallery, garden, and lounge. Toast to Milan with a chic cocktail.

Three stylish days in Milan? Expertly executed! As you whisper "Arrivederci" to this design deity, hold tight to memories of maestros, Milanese meals, and moments of moda. Eager for another escapade? Just say the word, dear traveler. Ciao for now! 🇮🇹💅👠

Naples

Espresso, Explorations, and the Echoes of Etna

Day 1: Antiquity, Art, and Authentic Pizza

MORNING: Naples National Archaeological Museum

Begin with a dive into some of the world's most impressive Greco-Roman artifacts. Pro tip: Don't challenge the statues to a staring contest.

LUNCH: L'Antica Pizzeria da Michele

For a pizza pilgrimage, it's a must. Brace for a queue, but the reward is the slice of your dreams.

AFTERNOON: Spaccanapoli

The street that literally splits Naples. Wander and absorb the unfiltered Neapolitan spirit.

EVENING: Piazza Bellini

Cap off the day with a drink amidst the mingling of locals and travelers, all serenaded by street musicians.

Character of the City:

Naples, a city with a character as rich as its ragù and as vibrant as its Vesuvian backdrop, is Italy's soul-stirring masterpiece. It's an urban canvas of chaotic streets, where history greets you at every turn, and life is lived as passionately as a Puccini opera.

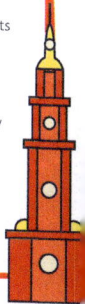

Day 2: Underground Mysteries and Sunset Vie

MORNING: Catacombs of San Gennaro

Explore the sacred silence and eerie beauty of this underground cemetery.

LUNCH: Sorbillo

Another legendary spot for pizza. If yesterday's
wasn't enough, today's will seal the deal.

AFTERNOON: Naples Underground (Napoli Sotterranea)

Delve 40 meters below to a labyrinth of ancient tunnels and cisterns.

EVENING: Castel Sant'Elmo

For sunset, ascend to this medieval fortress. The view is a panoramic
splendor of the city, sea, and Vesuvius.

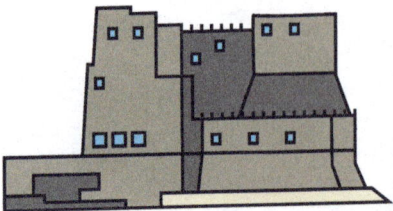

Day 3: Coastal Charms and Culinary Conquests

MORNING: Via San Gregorio Armeno

Known as 'Christmas Alley,' this street is famous for its artisanal nativity scenes and workshops. Yes, it's Christmas every day here.

LUNCH: La Campagnola

Savor some seafood and pasta, because when in Naples, you eat as the Neapolitans do.

AFTERNOON: Vomero Hill

Take the funicular up and explore the chic Vomero district, offering a different flavor of Neapolitan life.

EVENING: Bourbon Tunnel (Galleria Borbonica)

End your trip with a guided tour through this historic tunnel, a remnant of Naples' complex past.

As your 72 hours in Naples wind down, may your memories be as rich as the city's coffee, your spirit as fiery as Mount Vesuvius, and your heart as full as after a Neapolitan feast. Napoli isn't just a city; it's a living, breathing museum where every street corner tells a story. 🏛️⛰️🇮🇹

BORDEAUX

Bordeaux

A Weekend of Vineyards, Vistas, and Vivacious Vieux

Day 1: Boulevards, Bistros, and Bordeaux's Best

MORNING: Place de la Bourse & The Water Mirror

Start your exploration at this stunning square, reflecting 18th-century grandeur. Don't miss the Miroir d'eau, the world's largest reflecting pool, for that perfect photo op.

LUNCH: Marche des Capucins

The heart of Bordeaux's culinary scene. Indulge in oysters and a glass of crisp, local white wine.

Character of the City:

Welcome to Bordeaux, the world's wine capital, where elegance and edginess blend as seamlessly as a well-aged Merlot. This French jewel, nestled along the Garonne River, is a paradise for lovers of wine, history, and charming streets that tell tales as old as the vines.

AFTERNOON: Rue Sainte-Catherine

Stroll down Europe's longest pedestrian shopping street. A haven for shopaholics and window-shoppers alike.

EVENING: Le Bar a Vin

Nestled in the Bordeaux Wine Council building, sample a variety of regional wines without breaking the bank.

Day 2: Vineyards, Vistas, and Vintage Adventures

MORNING: **Saint-Emilion**

A short trip from the city, this UNESCO-listed wine village is straight out of a fairytale. Explore the vineyards, wine cellars, and quaint cobblestone streets.

LUNCH: **Hostellerie De Plaisance**

Enjoy a meal with a view in Saint-Émilion. The regional cuisine here is as breathtaking as the vista.

AFTERNOON: **Wine Tasting in Saint-Emilion**

Savor the world-renowned wines. From opulent reds to sparkling crémants, your palate is in for a treat.

EVENING: **Return to Bordeaux**

Enjoy a leisurely evening by the Garonne River, perhaps with a bottle of your favorite newfound wine.

Day 3: Galleries, Gardens, and Gastronomic Delights

MORNING: Musée d'Aquitaine

Delve into the region's history, from prehistoric times through the Middle Ages to the present day.

LUNCH: La Tupina

A rustic restaurant famed for traditional French cuisine cooked over an open fire. A must-try!

AFTERNOON: Jardin Public

Unwind in this lush public garden. It's perfect for a lazy stroll or a picnic with local cheeses and a fresh baguette.

EVENING: Darwin Ecosystem

A hub for eco-friendly businesses and a great spot for dinner. The atmosphere buzzes with innovation and creativity.

Three days in Bordeaux? Mission accomplished! As you bid "Au revoir" to this city of wine and wonder, savor the memories of each sip, sight, and stone. Ready for your next escapade? I'm here to guide you. Bon voyage! 🍷✈️🇫🇷

Lyon

Lights, Lyonnais Cuisine, and Labyrinthine Traboules

Day 1: Renaissance Romance, Riverside Rambles, and Ravishing Repasts

MORNING: VIEUX LYON (OLD LYON)

Begin your exploration in this UNESCO World Heritage site, strolling through narrow cobbled lanes and pastel-hued buildings. The Gothic Saint-Jean Cathedral is a must-see.

LUNCH: BOUCHON

Dive into Lyon's unique bouchon culture with a hearty lunch. Try the "quenelle" – a light, creamy fish dumpling that's a local specialty.

AFTERNOON: FOURVIERE HILL

Take the funicular to this hilltop district. Visit the majestic Basilica of Notre-Dame de Fourvière and enjoy panoramic views of the city.

EVENING: RIVERSIDE STROLL

Walk along the banks of the Saône, soaking in the city's tranquil beauty as the lights begin to twinkle.

CHARACTER OF THE CITY:

Embark on an enchanting journey through Lyon, France's gastronomic heart. This city, nestled at the confluence of the Rhône and Saône rivers, is a harmonious blend of Renaissance-rich history, vibrant urban culture, and culinary prowess. With its famed Fête des Lumières, silk weavers' secrets, and a labyrinth of traboules (passageways), Lyon promises a feast for the senses.

Day 2: Silk Weavers' Secrets, Sumptuous Markets, and Sublime Views

MORNING: CROIX-ROUSSE

This hill was the heart of Lyon's silk industry. Explore the traboules used by silk workers and discover hidden courtyards and murals.

LUNCH: LES HALLES DE LYON PAUL BOCUSE

Named after the city's most famous chef, this upscale market offers a variety of gourmet delights. It's an ideal spot for sampling local cheeses, charcuterie, and pastries.

AFTERNOON: LYON MUSEUM OF FINE ARTS (MUSEE DES BEAUX-ARTS)

Immerse yourself in one of France's largest art collections, housed in a stunning 17th-century former abbey.

EVENING:

PRESQU'ILE DISTRICT

Wander through this peninsula between the Rhône and Saône, dotted with shops, cafés, and lively squares like Place des Terreaux.

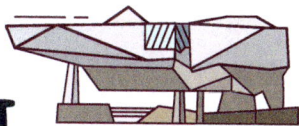

Day 3: Parks, Puppets, and Piquant Plates

MORNING: PARC DE LA TETE D'OR

Start with a relaxing morning in Lyon's largest urban park. Enjoy its lake, botanical garden, and zoo.

LUNCH: CAFE DES FEDERATIONS

Another chance to indulge in Lyonnais cuisine. Don't miss out on trying a "tarte aux pralines" for dessert.

AFTERNOON: GUIGNOL PUPPET SHOW

Catch a traditional puppet show, a fun and unique aspect of Lyonnais cultural heritage.

EVENING: CONFLUENCE MUSEUM (MUSEE DES CONFLUENCES)

End your visit at this futuristic museum at the confluence of Lyon's two rivers. Its exhibitions are as striking as its architecture.

Three days in Lyon? Mission deliciously accomplished! As you bid "Au revoir" to this city of lights and flavors, carry with you the tastes, tales, and traboules of your journey. Ready for more adventures? I'm here to guide you. Bon voyage! 🇫🇷 ✖ 🏛

Nice

Azure Seas, Artistic Allure, and Alluring Alleys

Day 1: Promenades, Paintings, and Panoramas

MORNING: Promenade des Anglais

Start your day with a stroll along this famous seafront boulevard. Feel the fresh sea breeze and soak in the stunning views of the Baie des Anges (Bay of Angels).

LUNCH: Cours Saleya Market

Meander through this lively market in the Old Town. Grab a socca (chickpea pancake) from a local vendor – it's a Niçois specialty!

AFTERNOON: Musee Matisse

Immerse yourself in the colorful world of Henri Matisse. Set in a 17th-century Genoese villa, the museum holds a vast collection of his works.

EVENIGHT: Castle Hill (Colline du Chateau)

As the day winds down, ascend to this panoramic viewpoint for a spectacular sunset over Nice and the Mediterranean.

Character of the City:

Welcome to Nice, the jewel of the French Riviera, where the allure of the deep blue Mediterranean meets the charm of a bustling city. With its blend of Italian influence, artistic heritage, and Belle Époque elegance, Nice is a delightful escape into a world of sun-soaked beaches, vibrant markets, and a relaxed, joie de vivre lifestyle.

Day 2: Artisanal Ambiance, Antique Alleys, and Azure Waters

MORNING: Vieux Nice (Old Town)

Wander the narrow, winding streets of the Old Town. The Italianate architecture and vibrant façades are a visual feast.

LUNCH: Le Safari

Sit in one of the bustling restaurants in the Old Town and savor local dishes like salade niçoise or ratatouille.

AFTERNOON: Nice's Beaches

Spend a relaxing afternoon on the pebbly shores of Nice's beaches. For a more secluded spot, try Coco Beach.

EVENING: Rue Bonaparte

Known as "Le Petit Marais", this trendy area is perfect for an evening of bar-hopping and discovering Nice's lively nightlife.

Day 3: Markets, Museums, and Mediterranean Magic

MORNING: Marche aux Fleurs

Start your day in the flower market, a riot of colors and fragrances. It's also a great place for picking up local artisanal products.

LUNCH: Chez Pipo

A local institution, enjoy a relaxing lunch here with a view of the sea. Try their famed pissaladière, a delicious onion tart.

AFTERNOON: Musee d'Art Moderne et d'Art Contemporain (MaMAC)

Explore modern and contemporary art, featuring works by Yves Klein and Andy Warhol, among others.

EVENING: Port of Nice

Conclude your trip with a stroll around the port, admiring the yachts and the blend of classic and modern architecture. Enjoy a final gourmet dinner at one of the portside restaurants.

Three days in Nice? A dream realized! As you bid "Au revoir" to this Riviera paradise, take with you memories of azure seas, artistic wanders, and the relaxed, sun-kissed spirit of Nice. Ready for your next adventure? I'm here to help. Bon voyage! 🎨🌊☀️

Glasgow

Gallantry, Gallus, and Grit in 72 Hours

Day 1: Grandeur, Galleries, and Gourmet Grub

MORNING: Kelvingrove Art Gallery and Museum

Kick off your exploration in this magnificent building.
From Dali's masterpieces to a Spitfire plane, it's a cultural feast.

LUNCH: Mother India's Cafe

Sample some of the city's best Indian cuisine with tapas-style dishes.

AFTERNOON: Glasgow School of Art

Admire Charles Rennie Mackintosh's architectural genius. Tip: Don't miss the Mackintosh House at the Hunterian Art Gallery nearby.

EVENING: West End

Wander through this bohemian neighborhood, filled with quirky shops, bars, and the picturesque Botanic Gardens.

CHARACTER OF THE CITY:

Welcome to Glasgow, the heart of Scotland's culture and creativity. A city of contrasts, where striking Victorian architecture meets innovative modern designs, Glasgow is a place where history and heritage vibrantly coexist with a dynamic contemporary arts scene. Known for its friendly locals, or 'Glaswegians', the city is a treasure trove of museums, galleries, and music venues, all set against the backdrop of the River Clyde.

Day 2: History, Haute Couture, and Hip Hangouts

MORNING: Riverside Museum and Tall Ship

Delve into Glasgow's shipbuilding past and explore the historic Glenlee ship moored outside.

LUNCH: The Gannet

Indulge in modern Scottish cuisine in this award-winning restaurant.

AFTERNOON: Buchanan Street and Style Mile

Experience Glasgow's shopping heart, with an array of high street and designer brands.

EVENING: King Tut's Wah Wah Hut

Catch some live music at this iconic venue – it's where Oasis were famously discovered!

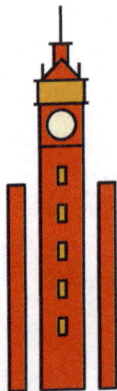

Day 3: Parks, Pubs, and Peculiarities

MORNING: **Pollok Country Park**

Start your day with a serene walk in Glasgow's largest park, and don't miss the Burrell Collection housed within.

LUNCH: **The Butterfly and the Pig**

Enjoy a hearty lunch in this quirky and cozy eatery.

AFTERNOON: **Glasgow Cathedral and Necropolis**

Explore this historic area, including the awe-inspiring St. Mungo's Cathedral and the adjacent Victorian cemetery.

EVENING: **Merchant City**

Finish your Glasgow adventure in this vibrant area known for its array of bars, restaurants, and buzzing nightlife.

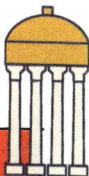

Three days in Glasgow will leave you with a lasting impression of a city that's rich in history, brimming with artistic flair, and buzzing with a unique energy. From its friendly locals to its cultural jewels, Glasgow is a city that invites you to dive deep into its charm and character.

Bucharest

Balkan Buzz, Belle Époque Beauty, and Bustling Boulevards in 72 Hours

Day 1: Historical Havens and Hearty Cuisine

MORNING: **Palace of the Parliament**

Begin your exploration with this colossal edifice, a legacy of Ceaușescu's rule. The sheer size of the building is a statement in itself.

LUNCH: **Caru' cu Bere**

Immerse yourself in Romanian culinary tradition in this legendary beer hall. Don't miss trying a plate of mici, grilled spicy meat rolls.

AFTERNOON: **Old Town (Lipscani)**

Wander through the charming streets of the Old Town, brimming with history, quaint shops, and cafés.

EVENING: **Strada Francez**

Dine in one of the ambient restaurants on this picturesque street, enjoying the blend of historical and contemporary Bucharest.

CHARACTER OF THE CITY:

Discover Bucharest, Romania's vibrant capital, where East meets West in a dance of architectural elegance and urban energy. Often dubbed "Little Paris" for its grand boulevards and Belle Époque buildings, Bucharest is a city of contrasts, merging its storied past with a lively, youthful spirit. From the remnants of its communist era to the thriving café culture and nightlife, Bucharest offers a captivating blend of history, culture, and entertainment.

Day 2: Art, Antiquities, and Artisanal Adventures

MORNING: ROMANIAN ATHENAEUM

Start your day with a visit to this stunning concert hall, a symbol of Romanian culture and arts.

LUNCH: THE ARTIST

This spot offers a modern take on Romanian cuisine, perfect for a culinary adventure.

AFTERNOON: NATIONAL MUSEUM OF ART OF ROMANIA

Explore the country's largest art collection, housed in the former royal palace.

EVENING: GRADINA EDEN

Spend your evening in this hidden garden bar, enjoying a relaxed atmosphere amidst trees and fairy lights.

Day 3: Parks, Palaces, and Party Vibes

MORNING: **Her str u Park**

Begin your day with a stroll or a boat ride in Bucharest's largest park, offering a serene escape from the urban bustle.

LUNCH: **Beraria H**

If you're a beer enthusiast, this is the place for you, offering a wide selection of local and international beers and hearty meals.

AFTERNOON: **Cotroceni Palace**

Discover the elegance of this historical palace, which also houses the Romanian Presidential residence.

EVENING: **Control Club**

Cap off your Bucharest adventure with a visit to this popular club, known for its vibrant music scene and lively atmosphere.

Three days in Bucharest will enchant you with its architectural splendor, rich history, and dynamic urban life. From the grandeur of its past to the buzzing energy of its present, Bucharest is a city that surprises and delights, offering a unique and memorable experience.

Thessaloniki

Byzantine Beauty, Bustling Boulevards, and Bountiful Bazaars

Day 1: Waterfront Wonders and Historical Haunts

MORNING: Aristotelous Square

Begin your Thessaloniki adventure at this iconic waterfront square, brimming with cafes and offering splendid views of the Thermaic Gulf.

LUNCH: Ladadika District

Head to this colorful, historic quarter for a mouthwatering meze lunch at one of the traditional tavernas.

AFTERNOON: White Tower

Explore the city's most famous landmark, offering panoramic views and a glimpse into its historical journey.

EVENING: Waterfront Promenade

Enjoy a leisurely evening stroll along the seafront, soaking in the vibrant atmosphere.

CHARACTER OF THE CITY:

Immerse yourself in Thessaloniki, Greece's vibrant cultural melting pot, blending its rich Byzantine and Ottoman history with a lively contemporary spirit. This seaside city, with its charming promenades, historic monuments, and spirited youth culture, offers a delightful exploration of the past and present. Known for its diverse cuisine, lively festivals, and warm hospitality, Thessaloniki is a treasure trove of experiences waiting to be discovered.

Day 2: Byzantine Brilliance, Artistic Alleys, and Gastronomic Galore

MORNING: CHURCH OF SAINT DEMETRIOS

Visit this stunning 7th-century church, dedicated to the city's patron saint, with its remarkable crypt and mosaics.

LUNCH: MODIANO MARKET

Indulge in fresh, local Greek produce and street food in this bustling market.

AFTERNOON: ANO POLI (UPPER TOWN)

Wander through the old city's cobbled streets, enjoying the traditional architecture and picturesque views.

EVENING: VALAORITOU DISTRICT

Experience Thessaloniki's modern pulse with an array of trendy bars and music venues.

Day 3: Museums, Markets, and Mediterranean Moments

MORNING: Archaeological Museum of Thessaloniki

Dive into the city's ancient Greek and Roman history with a visit to this renowned museum.

LUNCH: Agias Sofias Street

Choose from various cafes and eateries on this bustling street for a relaxing lunch.

AFTERNOON: Rotunda and Galerius Arch

Discover these impressive Roman-era monuments, a testament to Thessaloniki's rich historical tapestry.

EVENING: Ladadika

Return to this charming area for a final evening of delicious Greek dining and possibly some live music.

Three days in Thessaloniki will leave you enthralled with its blend of historical grandeur and modern vibrancy. As you depart, carry with you the memories of Byzantine wonders, culinary delights, and the warmth of Greek hospitality. Thessaloniki is a city that not only tells the tales of its past but also vibrantly lives in the present.

Printed in Dunstable, United Kingdom